T. Harry Williams

WITH BEAUREGARD IN MEXICO
is printed in a limited edition of 1,150
copies, of which 1,000 are for sale

This is copy number __498__

With Beauregard in Mexico

With

BEAUREGARD

The Mexican War

P. G. T.

Edited by

IN MEXICO

Reminiscences of
Beauregard

T. HARRY WILLIAMS

With illustrations by M. ETHEL BUVENS

Louisiana State University Press

For 'Uncle Harry'

Table of Contents

List of Maps

With Beauregard in Mexico

P. G. T. Beauregard in Mexico

MARCH–SEPTEMBER, 1847

ON December 17, 1852, First Lieutenant P. G. T. Beaure-gard, captain and major by brevet, of the Engineer Corps of the United States Army, put down his pen with a feeling of satisfaction. He had just finished writing an account of his experiences in the Mexican War; in accordance with the liter-ary style of the day he affixed a grand title to his manuscript: "Personal Reminiscences of an Engineer Officer During the Cam-paign in Mexico Under General Winfield Scott in 1847–8." As he finished his work, he glowed with the pride of author-ship. He thought that some time he would do more writing, per-haps compose a more general story of the war which he would call "General Reminiscences."

3

Beauregard in Mexico

Beauregard must have done his writing in odd hours that he squeezed from his duties as supervisor of defenses on the Louisiana Gulf Coast with headquarters in New Orleans. The motives that impelled a busy officer to turn to the unaccustomed task of literary composition are not hard to determine. They are evident in several letters which Beauregard wrote to friends, copies of which he filed with his copy of the "Reminiscences." Beauregard was a young man with a driving ambition. He confidently expected a call to greatness; it is hardly an exaggeration to say that he thought of himself as a man of destiny. His unconscious egotism was reflected in his remark that he would entitle a history of the war "General Reminiscences." He believed that he had played an important role in the operations in Mexico, a role so important that it should be put down on paper so that people would know what he had done. It would not be fair to conclude that he was deliberately setting out to ensure himself a place in history. He had, nevertheless, a strong sense of history, which remained with him throughout his entire life, and histories of the war or books dealing with it had appeared and others were in the making. It is not unjust to say that Beauregard hoped to get his services noted in some of the war books. In 1853 he sent a copy of his manuscript to John A. Quitman, who had been a division commander in Mexico and who was now an influential political figure in Mississippi. Quitman, who must have heard about the existence of the manuscript from Beauregard, had asked for a copy. He was having his biography prepared by J. F. H. Claiborne, and he thought Beauregard's account would aid Claiborne in writing the sections on the Mexican War. When the biography was published, it included excerpts from the "Reminiscences," without giving, however, any clear identification of Beauregard's manuscript or of its nature.[1]

[1] J. F. H. Claiborne, *The Life and Correspondence of John A. Quitman,* Vol. I (New York, 1860), Chapter XIII.

Introduction

But a more impelling and immediate reason than a desire for historical fame prompted Beauregard to turn author. He had come out of the war an embittered and unhappy man. He believed that he had not been treated fairly by his superiors, that he had not received the mention he deserved in the official reports, and that other officers had been given credit which should have gone to him. Although he had been awarded the brevets of captain and major, which meant that he had the grade without the pay, he felt that others who had not done as well as he had been put ahead of him on the promotion list. As he would brood over these imagined injustices over the years he would become more embittered, to a point where in 1856 he threatened to leave the army.[2] For some reason, he blamed General Scott for his misfortunes. He promised himself that when he wrote his general account of the war he would have something to say about Scott's errors in conducting the Mexican campaign. The lieutenant would teach the lieutenant-general!

It is not too fanciful to assume that Beauregard wrote his reminiscences partly to salve his bruised ego. In his own pages, at least, he would receive the recognition he had been denied in the reports. In one document, if in no other, the record would be put straight. But he did not write just to give himself comfort and reassurance. He intended his manuscript to be seen— by other officers and by influential civilians. He had his secretary make a number of copies, which he circulated among his friends. Apparently he thought that if his account reached enough people, it would enlarge his reputation. The men who ran the army would hear about it and would be impressed. Then he would receive the promotions that were justly his and the recognition that belonged to him as the officer who had shown General Scott how to capture Mexico City. He would realize the brilliant promise of his days at West Point, when as an

[2] See letters in Appendix.

honor student, he seemed destined to become one of the finest officers in the army.

Pierre Gustave Toutant-Beauregard knew he wanted to be a soldier when he was little more than a boy. When he announced his choice of a profession to his family, they were shocked, not because they disapproved of soldiers, but because he proposed to enter the United States Army. As good Creoles, they thought this was carrying cooperation with Americans pretty far. But they let him have his way, having learned from experience that it was impossible to move him once he had made up his mind.

Born in 1818 in St. Bernard Parish, just below New Orleans, a son of one of the aristocratic Creole families of south Louisiana, Beaurgard came into a world that was more French than American. Unlike most Creoles, however, his father believed in some contacts with outside culture. He sent Pierre to a school in New York operated by two former Frenchmen, brothers, who had served under Napoleon. From the old soldiers the boy received more than the technical education the father had wanted him to acquire. He found a hero—the great Corsican—upon whom he would model himself for the rest of his life, and he determined on a profession—the military— which he would follow in the army of the United States. Through the influence of his family he secured an appointment to West Point, entering in 1834 and, after compiling a brilliant record, graduating second in the class of 1838. At the academy, seeking to Americanize himself, he dropped the hyphen from his name; a few years later he deleted the Pierre and started signing himself "G. T. Beauregard."

After graduating he accepted a commission in the Engineer Corps, then regarded as the elite branch of the army. After serving briefly in posts in Rhode Island and Florida, he persuaded his superiors to assign him to service in Louisiana. In his native state his job was to supervise the construction of forts on the Gulf Coast and to study navigation conditions at the various mouths of the Mississippi. He was in Louisiana when the Mexican War started in May, 1846.

Like other young army officers, Beauregard was excited by the news that war had come, and, like the others, he wanted to get in it right away. These men had a natural desire to practice their profession under actual conditions, but in addition they saw in the war a chance to advance themselves. In the small peacetime army, absorbed with routine activities, promotions for the younger officers came with agonizing slowness; they promised to come more rapidly in the larger organization that would be required to fight a foreign war. To Beauregard and others like him, the war appeared as their first big opportunity, their first chance for fame.

For several months it seemed that the war was going to pass Beauregard by. Although he bombarded the Chief of the Engineer Department, Colonel Joseph G. Totten, with requests to be sent to General Zachary Taylor's army in Texas, he received no assignment. Soon Taylor crossed the Rio Grande and occupied a triangular area in notheastern Mexico. An important point in the seized area was the port city of Tampico on the eastern coast, which could be used as a base to supply the American forces. To render Tampico safe against a possible enemy attack, the Engineer Department decided to ring its land side with fortifications. Totten now remembered Beauregard and his applications for service; Beauregard's engineering talents could be employed at Tampico. He instructed the lieutenant to proceed to the town and take charge of the fort-building. Beauregard arrived early in December; he would work at his forts until he completed them in February. Then he was ordered by Totten to be ready to join the biggest offensive movement the government had as yet launched in the war.

The American high command had thought that Taylor's

victories would force the Mexicans to sue for peace on American terms. Instead they continued to fight and gave no indication that they were even thinking of peace. The American planners then produced a new and bolder design, one that was the joint product of President James K. Polk and General Scott, the ranking general in the army and its best soldier. An army under Scott's command, to be created by taking part of Taylor's forces and uniting them with troops from other theaters, was to be collected at Tampico. With this army Scott would strike at the heart of Mexico, its capital, Mexico City. From Tampico the navy would transport the force to the next point of rendezvous, the Lobos Islands, just off the coast, and from there to the port city of Vera Cruz, which would be seized and used as the army's base of supplies. From Vera Cruz the National Highway, an inviting avenue of invasion, ran west to Mexico City. Scott believed that the Mexicans would fight for their capital and that the defeat of their army and the occupation of the city would end the war.

In February, 1847, Scott came to Tampico to take command of his gathering forces and to complete the preparations for his movement. Scott was really a fine soldier. His plan was brilliantly conceived, and, for the most part, it would be brilliantly executed. With an army that never numbered more than 14,000 men and that sometimes sank to 9,000, he completed one of the most successful campaigns in American military annals, taking his army deep into the enemy country, winning a series of victories without suffering a serious reverse, and finally capturing the enemy capital to bring the war to a close with victory for his country.

Among the several elements that made up Scott's greatness was his realization that there were certain deficiencies in his military education. He had not attended West Point; indeed, he had had no formal military training whatsoever. And yet

8

Introduction

unlike many self-made soldiers, he valued education; in particular, he respected West Point and the students it turned out. He gathered West Pointers about him, knowing that they could provide him with the technical, specialized knowledge which he did not have.

The conflict with Mexico was the first American war in which an appreciable number of West Point graduates served in the armed forces. For the first time the military academy was able to furnish, through its products, a practical demonstration of the value of its training. In no previous war did American armies have in their organization as many trained officers as did the armies of Taylor and Scott. Nearly all of the general officers, the division, brigade, and regimental commanders, were men who had received no formal education. The West Pointers were active and made their contributions in the lower echelons of the infantry, artillery, and engineer services.

Scott esteemed all the West Point officers, and gave them generous praise in his reports. But one unit was closer to his heart and worked more closely with him than the others. This was the group of able young engineer officers, of which Beauregard was a member, usually known as the Engineer Company. The other members were Major John L. Smith, Captains Robert E. Lee and James L. Mason, and Lieutenants Zealous B. Tower, Isaac I. Stevens, Gustavus W. Smith, John G. Foster, and George B. McClellan. Scott employed the engineers in various important functions. Before making a forward movement, before fighting a battle, he had them make careful reconnaissances of the terrain and of the enemy positions. Often his tactical decisions were based on their information. On occasion he asked their advice even in forming strategic decisions. At a time when the army did not have a staff in the modern sense, the engineers constituted a kind of unofficial General Staff.

Beauregard in Mexico

From the Lobos Islands the navy transported Scott's army to Vera Cruz. The fleet approached the city on March 5, anchoring between a group of islands and Cape Anton Lizardo on the mainland. On the ninth the troops were landed on the beach below Vera Cruz. The landing was a model of careful planning and efficient execution—the first major joint amphibious operation of the United States Army and Navy.[3] It is at this point in Scott's campaign that Beauregard began his narrative.

After the army was ashore, Scott's first act was to collect his engineers and inspect the defenses of Vera Cruz. The commanding general decided that he could not risk his small army, numbering at that time about 10,000 men, in an assault against the walled town. Vera Cruz would have to be taken by siege. Siege operations as practiced by armies in the nineteenth century were based on the doctrines of the great French engineer, Vauban. First, the besiegers would try to completely invest the place under attack, blocking off all its lines of supply. Then they would mount batteries to pound the fortifications. The object of a siege was to move the artillery pieces ever closer to the target, finally to a point where the guns could demolish the walls or the infantry of the besiegers could rush over or through them. As the batteries advanced, field fortifications and trenches had to be constructed to protect the guns and to shelter infantry who would guard the pieces against sorties from the garrison. In a Vauban-type siege, good engineer officers were an absolute necessity. Without his engineers, Scott could not have captured Vera Cruz, unless he had chanced a bloody infantry assault that might have left his army too weak to continue operations. For the engineers the siege of almost

[3] Robert Selph Henry, *The Story of the Mexican War* (Indianapolis, 1950), 262.

three weeks duration was their first opportunity to apply their teachings under actual conditions.

After the army invested the town, the engineers went to work, studying possible weak spots in the fortifications, choosing sites for batteries, and superintending the erection of batteries. On several occasions Beauregard and other officers reconnoitered to within a few hundred yards of the walls to acquire information. Beauregard claimed in his narrative that three of the five batteries which finally reduced Vera Cruz were located on sites which he selected.

By March 22 the American batteries were so close to the city that they could not only batter the walls but fire into the city itself. The Mexican commander now realized that it was hopeless to continue his resistance, and on the twenty-ninth he surrendered the town. The officers of the Engineer Company believed that it was their skills which had enabled Scott to take Vera Cruz with but a trifling loss of life. Scott and his principal officers seemed to agree with them, for the official reports to Washington glowed with praise for the engineers. Colonel Totten, Chief of the Engineer Department, commended each officer by name. Beauregard was glad to have his name mentioned in the reports, but he was angered by Totten's account. The chief had given equal commendation to all the engineers, and Beauregard felt that as the officer who had located most of the batteries he should have received special citation and perhaps a promotion. Here was the beginning of a feeling of bitterness that would increase during the war and endure for years after its close.

Scott kept the army in Vera Cruz only long enough to organize the town as a base. Anxious to get the troops out of the low country before the hot season struck, he sent his divisions marching west on the National Highway. As the army advanced, Scott remained in Vera Cruz to complete his preparations. Beauregard accompanied the division of General Robert Patterson, to which he was attached as engineer officer. On April 11–12, the vanguard of the army, led by the divisions of Patterson and General David E. Twiggs, emerged from the plains into the mountains and found the main Mexican field army, under the command of General Santa Anna, barring the line of march. Santa Anna had arranged his forces in a strong position. His right rested on a river; north of the highway was a hill called Cerro Gordo, on which Santa Anna had mounted batteries. He was confident that he could halt any American advance on the main road with murderous losses.

Twiggs, who did not know much about the science of war, nevertheless knew a strong position when he saw one. In an effort to discover if the Mexican line had a weak spot, he had sent some officers to reconnoiter the enemy left. When Beauregard arrived, he, as the most experienced engineer officer present, took charge of the reconnaissance. With one of Twiggs's officers and an escort, he followed a path that led around Cerro Gordo; and going farther than Twiggs's scouts had gone, a mile in rear of the Mexican line, he came to a hill north of Cerro Gordo called Atalaya. Surveying the terrain from there, he decided that Cerro Gordo could be carried and the Mexicans flanked out of their line. He so recommended to Twiggs when he returned.

On the basis of Beauregard's information, which certainly was far from complete, Twiggs resolved to attack the Mexicans. He proposed to Patterson and the other general officers who were present that two divisions assail the enemy front while his own division struck Cerro Gordo. Although the other officers assented, Patterson had doubts about the plan. He asked Beauregard what he thought of it. The lieutenant said that it might succeed but that he preferred a different mode of attack, with the main blow falling on Cerro Gordo. Patterson agreed and suggested that Beauregard should go to Twiggs and present his views. As ready then as he was in the later days of the Confederacy to lecture his superiors on strategy, Beauregard went to the general and argued for a change in plan. Twiggs refused to give up the attack, in a scene which Beauregard described vividly in his manuscript. Fortunately for the American cause, Twiggs did call off his offensive. Hearing that Scott was about to arrive, he concluded that maybe the commanding general should be allowed to handle the battle.

Scott, when he resumed command, was appalled that his subordinates had considered attacking the Mexican position. Always conscious of the necessity of conserving lives in his small army, he sought whenever possible to achieve his objective by a flanking movement instead of risking a frontal assault. So now he discarded Twiggs's plan, and looked for a way around the enemy left so that he could pass a force to Santa Anna's rear. Beauregard's reconnaissance pointed a possible route, which Scott followed up. He directed that further scouts be made. On April 15 Beauregard, Lee, and other officers followed Beauregard's trail to Atalaya. While the others ascended the hill, Beauregard went on alone almost to the base of Cerro Gordo. Then a fever which he had contracted at Vera Cruz recurred, and he had to return to camp. For the next few days he was so sick that he could not go about his duties. His illness was a terrible piece of bad luck. The reconnaissance which he had begun was taken over and completed by Lee, who found a path by which a force could move to the Mexican rear. Beauregard missed the credit for finishing the reconnaissance, and he missed a chance to distinguish himself at the battle of Cerro Gordo on the eighteenth, when Scott turned the enemy left and won the field.

After the battle Beauregard found further evidence to bolster his belief that his superiors were not noticing him properly and were even disposed to deal unfairly with him. Scott, in his report, commended all the engineers. He was careful to say that the reconnaissance begun by Beauregard was completed by Lee; nevertheless, he singled out Lee for special praise. Beauregard burned with anger. He thought that he should have received credit at least equal to Lee's. Lee had discovered little that he did not already know, Beauregard fumed. It would not be the last time he would resent his Virginia comrade or think that Lee was receiving accolades which should be his.

Hardly pausing after Cerro Gordo, Scott drove the army on to Jalapa and then to Mexico's second largest city, Puebla, which was reached on May 15. At Puebla, Scott stopped for almost three months to organize his forces for the final push and to wait for reinforcements. During the long pause, the engineers collected information on the roads leading into the enemy capital and made sketches of both for Scott's use. Not until August 7 did the army leave Puebla for the last lap of the great march. Five days later it emerged from the mountains at Ayotla, and the excited soldiers saw the Valley of Mexico below them.

Ayotla was about twenty miles from Mexico City on the National Highway, which ran straight to the capital on a causeway between lakes and marshes. Commanding the road was a high hill known as El Penon. Two other possible routes were open to Scott. To the north a long, circuitous road skirted the northern shore of Lake Texcoco before reaching Mexico City. To the south a shorter road, which the Americans supposed to be in bad condition and possibly impassable, traversed the southern shores of Lakes Chalco and Xochimilco and came out south of the city. Santa Anna, who had not fought since Cerro Gordo, was known to be in the vicinity in force.

Introduction

Scott naturally preferred to move, if possible, on the direct middle route, but he feared that Santa Anna must have seen the obvious and fortified El Penon. In such case, the shortest road might be the most dangerous one. As he always did in a crisis, Scott called on his engineers. He instructed them to reconnoiter the road ahead, to determine the strength of El Penon, and to find out if the other two roads were usable. Beauregard was one of a group which explored the northern route. Later he and Lee worked along the shore of Chalco and secured information that the southern road was in better shape than had been supposed. As a result of the reconnaissances, the engineers reported to Scott that El Penon was crowned with artillery and that it could be taken only with heavy losses because the army would be largely confined to the causeway as it attacked. Immediately Scott decided to resort to his favorite flanking tactics. He would bypass El Penon by taking the southern road, which because of the information supplied by Lee and Beauregard and because of a scout made by an artillery officer, Colonel James Duncan, he believed to be passable.

The army swung out south of the lakes, heading for San Agustin, directly south of Mexico City, from where Scott intended to drive north at the capital. Scott's movement, however, was only a partial success. He had turned Santa Anna out of El Penon, but the Mexican commander had pulled back and now confronted Scott at San Antonio, a short distance above San Agustin. The situation was much the same as it had been. If the Americans advanced, they would have to travel a narrow causeway covered by artillery fire. Again Scott decided he would have to flank the enemy, and again he called on the engineers to devise a way to do it.

He sent one group north to reconnoiter the road to San Antonio. Lee and Beauregard he dispatched west across a huge lava bed called the Pedregal, charged with the mission of determining if the army, or a part of it, could cross the molten rocks and reach a road on the other side running north. If the Americans could get on this San Angel road, they could flank Santa Anna out of San Antonio. On the night of August 18 the two officers reported that they had found a path that could be built into a road.

The next day Scott set the troops of Twiggs and General Gideon J. Pillow to constructing a road. As the infantry labored, the engineers directed the work, conducted batteries into position, and explored toward the Mexican positions on the far side of the Pedregal. At intervals the road-building was halted by the attacks of Mexican troops stationed near the villages of Contreras and Padierna on the San Angel road. Finally the American officers on the scene decided to stop these assaults by taking the offensive themselves and storming the enemy works. Without anybody planning it exactly that way, a full-scale battle was about to develop.

As the Americans advanced, they found the going rough because the Mexicans were in superior numbers and were receiving reinforcements down the San Angel road. From his headquarters at San Agustin, Scout could see what was happening. To succor his men, he ordered more troops over the Pedregal. One of the newly arrived generals, George Cadwalader, told Beauregard to go back and ask Scott for more help. Disappointed that he was going to miss another battle, Beauregard started out. Before going far, he met General Persifor F. Smith, who was on his way to the front where as the ranking officer on the field he would assume command. For both men the meeting was fortuitous. Beauregard wanted to stay on the scene, and Smith needed an engineer officer. The general took Beauregard with him.

After examining the Mexican position in company with Beauregard and Lee, Smith resolved upon an attack the next day, August 20, with the engineers guiding the columns to the rear of the Mexican camp. As the troops advanced in the early hours of the morning, Beauregard accompanied Smith at the head of the lead brigade. The movement caught the Mexicans completely by surprise, and they fled northward up the San Angel road, with the Americans in hot pursuit. At the same time Scott advanced his force at San Agustin, and Santa Anna, to escape being enveloped, had to abandon San Antonio and fall back to Churubusco. Scott, appreciating the magnitude of his victory, exploited it to the fullest. He ordered his exuberant troops on to Churubusco immediately. The Americans won their second victory of that hard-fought day when they stormed the new Mexican lines and drove Santa Anna's disorganized army into the defenses of the capital.

Beauregard had reason to be well satisfied with his part in the events of August 20. Smith, recognizing his services, had accorded him the honor of bearing the news of the victory at Contreras to Scott. All the reports praised his skill and gallantry, and as a tangible reward he was given the brevet of captain. But more satisfying to him was the fact that he had been on the inside of things—he had conducted vital reconnaissances, he had helped Smith plan the battle. He could feel important. And he certainly knew what had happened in the fighting. His account of these engagements is one of the clearest and fullest penned by a participant.

After Churubusco Scott prepared to move on Mexico City itself. At this point Santa Anna shrewdly asked for a truce, hinting that he might be willing to terminate the war. Scott, knowing that his government was anxious to conclude a peace treaty, agreed. Both sides pledged not to build up their strength during the negotiations. Scott soon discovered, however, that Santa Anna was not keeping his word; the Mexican commander was using the truce as a breathing space in which to reorganize his defenses. Irritated that he had been deceived so transparently, Scott broke off the talks and resumed hostilities.

As the American commander surveyed the terrain in front of Mexico City, he realized that he faced a difficult military problem. The capital stood on high ground surrounded by marshes and approached by causeways, three from the south and two from the west. Near the city's walls fortified *garitas* or gates guarded each approach. The roads from the south offered the most direct route, but the extensive marshes would confine the Americans to the roads where they would be subject to a killing artillery fire. The roads from the west were wider and the ground here was higher, which meant that the attackers would have more room in which to maneuver, but here too was the great fortress of Chapultepec, which would be in the rear of the Americans as they advanced. Whereas today such a position would be bypassed or contained, according to the military theories of the nineteenth century it would have to be taken—if Scott came in from the west.

At first Scott thought he would use the southern approaches. Early in September he had the engineers out reconnoitering every route, examining the condition of the roads, and spying out the defenses of the *garitas*. On one occasion, in a night scout, Beauregard almost reached one of the gates.

After all the reconnaissances, Scott was still undecided as to which route he should take. On September 11 he called a council of his principal officers and the engineers in the church at the village of Piedad to settle the issue. Stating that he had not arrived at a final decision, the commanding general explained the advantages and disadvantages of each route, and ended by saying he inclined to the western approach. One of the division generals spoke in favor of the southern route, and another said he would like to hear from the engineers. Smith, Lee, and two other engineers arose and advocated attacking

18

from the south. Their testimony, especially Lee's, had great weight. Four generals now said they agreed with the engineers, and it was evident that the council would vote for the southern approach. At this point several people asked Beauregard, who had come in late, why he did not give his views. Scott now saw Beauregard sitting in a corner, and he asked the lieutenant to speak.

Beauregard had apparently come to the council prepared to give his opinions. He presented a long, reasoned, and technical argument to support the western route. He had scouted the southern approaches thoroughly, he said, and he knew that their defenses were too strong to be carried. The Mexicans would expect an attack here at their strongest point and, he continued in a classroom style, in war one should never do what the enemy wishes you to do. Using a jargon acquired at West Point and from his reading of Napoleon's campaigns, he told his fascinated auditors that the best way to take a city was to feint an attack in one quarter and deliver a real one at another point. Seize Chapultepec, he advised, and move from it as a pivot on any part of Mexico City. The generals, many of whom were civilians in peacetime life, were impressed when he finished. So was Scott, who arose and announced that the attack would be delivered on Chapultepec and the western gates. It was undoubtedly Beauregard's greatest moment of the war.

His mind made up, Scott moved quickly. On September 11 the American batteries opened a concentrated fire on Chapultepec, and on the next day he launched an infantry assault on the fortress. In the attack Beauregard was supposed to guide Pillow's division, but actually he went where he pleased and did what he wanted. He had resolved that morning to be among the first to enter the works and to tear down the Mexican flag. As the troops went forward, he joined the Voltigeur unit of his future Confederate comrade, Lieutenant Colonel Joseph E. Johnston.

Crossing the parapet with the first storming parties, he looked for a way to the top of the walls so that he could seize the flag. He finally found a stairs, but upon emerging from it he saw to his great disappointment another officer hauling down the enemy emblem.

As the defeated Mexicans fled from Chapultepec toward the capital, Scott sent orders to his generals to advance toward the city by any available route. Several of them had already started to move, hoping to acquire the glory of being the first to enter Mexico City. Beauregard joined the division of John A. Quitman, who had lost his engineer officer and who welcomed Beauregard's proffer of service. The division advanced on a broad avenue which entered the city at Belen *garita*. As Beauregard reconnoitered the road for Quitman, he fell in a canal and twice was slightly wounded.

By dark Quitman had reached and stormed the *garita,* but he found his farther progress barred by fire from an old building known as the Citadel. He then decided to retire to the *garita* for the night and resume his advance in the morning. When morning came, the Americans saw a white flag flying from the Citadel. As Beauregard understood Spanish, he went forward to find the meaning of the flag. At the Citadel a lone Mexican officer informed him that the Mexicans had evacuated the city and that he had been left at this post to surrender it. Politely he asked Beauregard for a receipt. Beauregard refused, with a dramatic, theatrical statement. In describing the incident in his narrative, he saw the obvious humor in the Mexican's request, but being a young man who took himself seriously, not the humor in his reply.

Sensing that the disappearance of any opposition would enable him to grasp the honor of being the first into the capital, Quitman ordered his division to march to the Grand Plaza in the center of the city. When they reached it, the exultant Quitman told Beauregard to ride to Scott with the news. Beauregard found the general with another division entering the city on the San Cosme road.

For his services in the attack on Chapultepec, Beauregard received the brevet of major. He was, nevertheless, still bitter and still convinced that Scott had not treated him fairly. Scott, in his report of the entire campaign, gave great but equal credit to all the engineer officers. Beauregard thought that he should have received special mention for supporting the commanding general's views at the Piedad council.

Nor was his opinion of Scott as a general completely favorable. He conceded that Scott was the best general of the war, but he was not Beauregard's ideal of a soldier. Beauregard, before the war, had acquired certain rigid ideas about the art of warfare, derived primarily from his reading of Napoleon and Jomini. There were fixed rules, he believed, which must always be followed. Scott had departed from the rules, which shocked Beauregard and also puzzled him, for according to the rules Scott should have lost. Beauregard was inclined to ascribe his success to luck.

Beauregard did not study Scott's generalship or learn anything from the general's brilliant strategy, as Lee undoubtedly did. He entered the war with a belief that battles should be fought in conformity to a fixed pattern, and he left it with the same conviction. In short, his Mexican War experience indicated that he could not easily adjust his thinking to new conditions or easily improvise new ways of war. This characteristic of his military personality he would retain throughout his career. It was the greatest weakness in an otherwise able and potentially brilliant soldier.[4]

[4] This account of Beauregard's Mexican War service is largely based on Chapter II of my *P. G. T. Beauregard: Napoleon in Gray* (Baton Rouge, 1955), which contains in the footnotes a listing of the major

Beauregard in Mexico

The original manuscript of Beauregard's "Reminiscences" is in the Missouri Historical Society, St. Louis. I examined it a number of years ago when I was doing research for a biography of Beauregard. At that time I was impressed with its value as a source account of the Mexican War. Its existence seemed to be almost unknown to historians; at least, no significant part of the material in the narrative had been incorporated into books dealing with the war. I decided then that some day I would like to edit the manuscript for publication, thus making it generally available to scholars. After completing my biography, I asked Mr. Charles Van Ravenswaay, the director of the Society, for permission to place the manuscript in book form. He readily consented, and generously provided me with a typed copy. To him and his staff I am indebted for many kindnesses and much help.

I have reproduced the manuscript almost exactly as Beauregard wrote it. A few editorial liberties were taken with the purpose of achieving a clearer and more readable document. I have modernized some of his capitalizations and punctuation forms, I have spelled out many of his abbreviations, I have broken up long paragraphs into shorter ones, and I have corrected misspelled words and names. Beauregard was a fairly literate individual, and he probably would have made many of these alterations himself if he had intended his narrative to be published. In the footnotes I have tried to supply enough information to identify for the reader the important persons and places mentioned in the manuscript.

sources on the war and Beauregard's part in it. The best secondary works on the Mexican War, all of which contain excellent background material on Scott's campaign, are Henry's book, cited above; Justin H. Smith, *The War with Mexico,* 2 vols. (New York, 1919); Charles W. Elliott, *Winfield Scott: The Soldier and the Man* (New York, 1937); and Douglas Southall Freeman, *R. E. Lee,* Vol. I (New York, 1934).

Introduction

As a source document, Beauregard's narrative possesses a number of virtues. It has zest, freshness, and readability. His descriptions of certain operations, notably Contreras and Chapultepec, are unusually vivid and complete to have been written by a junior officer, and compare with the best accounts of those battles. In general, except where he was trying to exaggerate his own exploits, Beauregard wrote with an accuracy not often found in reminiscent records. This was because he put down his story soon after the events occurred, while they were still sharp in his mind, and because he based much of what he said on a brief diary or journal which he had kept in the war.[5]

Documents like Beauregard's narrative are of interest to historical scholars for two reasons. First, they provide information about the Mexican War and its battles and leading figures. Certainly a biographer of Scott or of any one of his generals would find much that was rewarding in what Beauregard wrote. Second, and perhaps more important, such records shed light on the military education and experience of the young officers who became the generals of the Civil War. For most of these men, the war with Mexico was the only important military event which they participated in before 1861. It was a training-school for the later and larger conflict. Biographers of the Northern and Southern generals have realized the importance of the Mexican War, but often they have had trouble tracing their subjects through it because of the relatively scanty records that have survived. The recollections or letters of one officer will inevitably tell something about the activities of other officers with whom he was associated. Such information is one of the contributions of the published letters of Robert Anderson and Ephraim Kirby Smith and the published diary of George B.

[5] This document is in the Beauregard Papers, in the Division of Manuscripts, Library of Congress.

McClellan.[6] It is hoped that Beauregard's reminiscences will occupy a place with these and other sources of the war that gained the United States an empire.

T. HARRY WILLIAMS

[6] Robert Anderson, *An Artillery Officer in the Mexican War* (New York, 1911); E. J. Blackwood (ed.), *To Mexico with Scott: Letters of Captain E. Kirby Smith to His Wife* (Cambridge, 1917); William Starr Myers (ed.), *The Mexican War Diary of George B. McClellan* (Princeton, 1917). Other interesting personal narratives are Raphael Semmes, *Service Ashore and Afloat During the Mexican War* (Cincinnati, 1851); John R. Kenley, *Memoirs of a Maryland Volunteer* (Philadelphia, 1873); and George C. Furber, *The Twelve Months Volunteer* (Cincinnati, 1849).

The Siege of Vera Cruz
MARCH 9–29, 1847

AT 12 h. M. on the 9th of March, 1847, the fleet of trans-
ports having all arrived at Cape Anton Lizardo—the
wind being favorable for the movement towards Vera Cruz
—the signal for weighing anchor was made on board of the flag
ship the *Massachusetts* and we arrived at about 2 h. P. M. in
rear of the Island of Sacrificios, where the necessary prelimi-
naries were made for landing immediately. At 4 h. the First
Division under General Worth started in one of the surf-boats
for the shore—presenting one of the finest spectacles I ever
witnessed. It was afterwards followed by the Second Division
under General Patterson, and then by the Third or reserve under
General Twiggs, the whole disembarkation being completed

before 12 h. that night—the enemy offering no opposition.[1]

Early on the morning of the 10th we took our line of march to circumvallate the City of Vera Cruz, driving in at the same time the enemy's forces which had come out and occupied the sand-hills around it, with the apparent intention of opposing our movements. Worth's right rested on the beach— Patterson's rested on Worth's left and then Twiggs formed on Patterson's left to the beach on the other side of the city. From the difficulties of the ground the investment was not however completed until the 18th. In the meantime the Engineers (eleven of us) were diligently employed reconnoitering as close to the city as practicable, to determine the point of attack and the position of our batteries, etc. As a matter of course, I will not here enter into all the details of the operations of the siege, which, although interesting to an officer of Engineers, would but render this narration rather too voluminous.

About the time of opening the trenches, Captain Lee[2] and myself returning late in the evening from a reconnoissance in front of our advanced pickets, which in the meantime had been withdrawn, as they were every night, we stumbled suddenly, as we issued from a thick undergrowth of chaparral into a

[1] In his manuscript Beauregard used the symbol "h." to indicate the hour of the day when a particular event occurred. In the first sentence "12 h. M." means that the movement started about noon. General Winfield Scott had first rendezvoused his army at the Lobos Islands; the second rendezvous was at Cape Anton Lizardo, two hundred miles farther south and a little below Vera Cruz, an anchorage between the mainland and a cluster of islands. From the anchorage the army was landed near Vera Cruz in a well-planned and skillfully-executed operation. The division generals referred to are William J. Worth, Robert Patterson, and David E. Twiggs.

[2] Robert E. Lee, the commander of the Army of Northern Virginia in the Civil War. The reader of this narrative will note that Beauregard felt a certain sense of rivalry with Lee, a feeling that he carried over into the larger war of the 1860's.

small open spot, upon some one who hailed us hurriedly, and before we had fairly time to answer his challenge, he fired upon us at *"brule pourpoint,"* not being at the time more than three or four paces from us; we were both blinded and stunned by the explosion; but before he had time to observe the effect of his shot, he was disarmed and completely in our power! For fearing he might have been armed with a revolver, at one spring we had grasped him and disarmed him. We then discovered that he was a soldier belonging to Captain Brooks' artillery company,[3] which was that day on *piquet* duty, and as he then pretended, was in search of his company, having lost his way in the chaparral; but we strongly suspected that he was neither more nor less than a deserter, then on his way to the City of Vera Cruz, which was not over 1,000 yards from us. We took him back to his company and never heard what became of him afterwards.

During the siege at Vera Cruz and in fact throughout the whole campaign, it was generally considered by the Engineer officers, that they were more exposed to being shot by our own advanced *piquets* or sentinels, on returning at night from their reconnoissances, than by the enemy's, especially when operating in front of the Volunteer divisions—and it was customary with us whenever approaching the positions which we knew were occupied by them, to give timely notice of our approach by exclaiming "don't shoot, we are American officers."[4]

On the afternoon of the 17th I was ordered by the Chief Engineer to go with a detachment of sappers and miners, com-

[3] Captain Horace Brooks, Second Artillery.

[4] Nearly all of the young regular officers who wrote about the Mexican War spilled pots of ink detailing the deficiencies of the volunteers. Beauregard, on the contrary, devotes but little space to the volunteers and is comparatively mild in his strictures. From this it may be inferred that he was modern-minded enough to realize that modern wars would have to be fought with "citizen" soldiers.

manded by Lieutenants Smith and Foster (or McClellan) [5] to lay out a battery of four (or six) guns toward the right of the city and within about 450 yards of its works. When I arrived on the spot, which was indicated to me by one of the above named officers, as the one selected that morning for that object, I found the position such an isolated and advanced one, exposed to such a heavy fire from the batteries of the city and the Castle of San Juan de Ulloa, that after considerable hesitation, I determined to go back to the encampment to explain my objections to the Chief Engineer and obtain further orders on the subject. About that time the enemy having had a glimpse of us through the chaparral and bushes which were our only protection, opened upon us with grape and round shots, and hastened considerably our retreat. We, however, soon found good cover in a break of the ridge on which we were moving and it struck me at the time as offering all the advantages of a good position for a mortar battery—and as it was not yet dark, I concluded that before returning to camp, I would perhaps be able to select other positions from which the Chief Engineer would be able to replace the one which I had thought proper not to mark out; so with the assistance of Lieutenant Smith, by sundown, I had chosen three others besides the one already spoken of, one of these being, we thought, an excellent site for a gun battery.[6]

[5] The Chief Engineer was Colonel Joseph G. Totten. The engineer officers named are G. W. Smith, John G. Foster, and George B. McClellan. Smith, a lifelong friend of Beauregard's, became a Confederate general in the Civil War, and served for a period under Beauregard's command. Foster and McClellan were generals in the Union service, the latter commanding the Army of the Potomac in 1861–62.

[6] Here Beauregard inserted a note saying that since writing the above he had learned that Totten had previously visited the position Beauregard had marked out for a battery and had indicated it would be a good site.

We then returned to camp where we arrived at dark, and reported to Colonel Totten the facts as above stated; he at first appeared surprised at my conduct; but soon gave me to understand that I might perhaps be right and that the next day he would go with Lieutenant Smith and myself to examine these new positions. This was accordingly done and I had the joy and satisfaction to find that they had met with his approbation, excepting one of the rear positions for a mortar battery, which had only been recommended in case one of the others in front had been found too near the city.

Those adopted were afterwards called mortar batteries No. 1 and 2, and gun battery No. 4—which were principally instrumental in reducing the city.

Preparations were then made to break ground that night (the 18th), and in the afternoon these batteries, with the parallel joining the first and last ones and passing in front of the cemetery, were staked out by Captain Lee, myself, Lieutenant Tower,[7] and the officers of the Sapper Company. Mortar battery No. 3 adjacent to and on the left of the cemetery, along the parallel, was selected by the Chief Engineer on the 20th. In the meantime the position of another 6-gun battery (No. 5) was selected (I believe) by the Chief Engineer or Captain Lee, and being afterwards armed with naval guns and defended by naval officers and sailors, was called the "Naval battery" and was noted for the rapidity and accuracy of firing.

Batteries 1, 2, and 3 opened against the city at 4 h. P. M. on the 22nd, No. 5 opened on the 24th and No. 4, in consequence of an accident happening to its parapet, did not open its fire until 8 h. A. M. on the 25th.

On the 24th a remarkable occurrence took place at mortar battery No. 3. Whilst I was busily employed constructing the platforms of gun battery No. 4, about 200 yards from the first

[7] Zealous B. Tower.

one, I heard in its direction a tremendous explosion which made me suppose its magazine had blown up. I repaired to the spot immediately and found Captain Arnold, his assistant Lieutenant Shields [8] and the men at one of the mortars, just picking themselves up considerably bruised and stunned but no one seriously hurt; the mortar having disappeared from its bed; its iron bed or chassis lying bottom up near its platform. As soon as Captain Arnold had sufficiently recovered from the shock, his face being slightly burnt, he informed me that just as the quick match of his mortar had been fired and whilst they were waiting for the explosion, a shell thrown from the city had struck in the angle formed by the mortar and its iron bed, breaking off a small piece of its under lip, the two explosions being almost simultaneous! His mortar had been thrown about twenty feet into the air—and it was then lying entirely outside of the battery, at least twenty yards to the rear of its original position! Its place had to be supplied with another one, taken from the Ordnance Department on the beach.

On the morning of the 25th a flag of truce was received offering to surrender the city, which put a stop to the firing on both sides, and on the 29th the terms of capitulation having been agreed upon, the city and castle surrendered, and we took possession of both on the morning of that day.

Thus, out of the five batteries which reduced the City of Vera Cruz, I had the honor (with Lieutenant G. W. Smith) to select the position of three of them! During the siege, one or two other batteries were established along our parallel, but they never opened. Now, in his report of that siege, what does the Chief Engineer, who ought, above all, to be extremely jealous of the reputation of his subordinate officers, say? "That all his officers behaved so well and did their duty so faithfully and zealously that it would be invidious to distinguish between

[8] Lewis G. Arnold; Hamilton L. Shields.

30

them." Without wishing to detract one iota from the reputation of my brother officers, who during that siege displayed constantly that activity, intelligence and gallantry for which they are so well renowned (conspicuous amongst them, however, were Captain Lee and Lieutenant McClellan), have I not the right, if not to complain, at any rate to feel surprised and pained at his lack of memory in this instance? If the thing was not very important in itself, yet to me, it was "more than my all"; for I had done there more than my legitimate duty, not only in selecting the positions of those batteries, but especially in condemning one *which I had received orders to mark out!*

History tells us that on one occasion, the establishment of a battery stamped a young officer of artillery as a very promising one in the eyes of his superiors! [9] and although far from pretending to such a high aspiration and not wishing in the least to establish a comparison between us, I was certainly entitled on that occasion, if not to a brevet, at any rate, to at least a passing notice in the official reports of the Chief Engineer!

[9] The historical reference is to Napoleon at the siege of Toulon.

The Battle of Cerro Gordo
APRIL 8–18, 1847

ON the 8th of April, Twiggs's division having Lieutenant Tower as engineer officer, left Vera Cruz for Cerro Gordo, where it arrived on the 11th. It may be well to remark here, that nothing definite was at the time known of the position of the enemy's forces—a report merely existing that we would likely encounter them at some point of the road in advance of Jalapa. Patterson's division of volunteers, to which I was attached at his own desire as Engineer officer, left Vera Cruz on the 9th, and arrived at Cerro Gordo at about noon on the 13th, where I found that Lieutenant Tower, accompanied by Captain Johnston, Topographical Engineers,[10] was making a reconnoissance in front of the right of the enemy's line of works—the latter

[10] This officer is Joseph E. Johnston, who later became a lieutenant

officer being about that time severely wounded by a fire of grape from the battery they were examining. Lieutenant Brooks [11] (General Twiggs's aide) than whom there is not a better or more gallant officer in the service, had also made a partial reconnoissance of the path leading from the main road (at about 800 yards from the enemy's advanced position) to the right of it, by which these positions, it was thought, could be avoided and the one of Cerro Gordo could be reached at once.

Lieutenant Brooks, as I was informed by himself in person, had reconnoitered about one-half of the path towards the hill of Cerro Gordo. I prepared that evening a rough sketch of the whole ground from the information which I had obtained of Lieutenants Tower and Brooks, Captain Drum [12] and others. Early on the morning of the 13th we started to complete the reconnoissance of the preceding day, Lieutenant Brooks generously offering to show me the way as far as he had gone along that mule path already spoken of; but he continued with me as far as I went that day. His offer was accepted, and we were accompanied, at his own request, by Captain Ayers, Third Artillery,[13] and had as an escort three or four companies of infantry.

When we arrived at the junction of that path with the main road, I left there the whole escort, except one company, which I distributed along it to the best advantage as we advanced, to protect us from a surprise in our rear; at the same time studying the general topography of the country so as to be able to make good our retreat in some other direction, in case of a sudden attack in our rear. We advanced cautiously and slowly,

---

colonel and the commander of a detachment of the Voltigeur Regiment. See note 33.

[11] W. T. H. Brooks.

[12] Simon H. Drum, Fourth Artillery.

[13] George W. Ayers.

on account of the difficulty to find our way, as the path had soon become entirely obliterated. When we had arrived at the foot of the hill immediately in front of the Cerro Gordo hill, called Atalaya, I left there the rest of my escort. We then ascended its steep slopes, only taking with us four or five sharp shooters, to protect us in the event of our finding an enemy's *piquet* on its crest; but we were fortunate enough to find it unoccupied, and we remained there an hour or two reconnoitering from our elevated position the whole country around us. We were then at least one mile in the rear of the enemy's front line of works. The Cerro Gordo hill was then occupied only by about two or three companies of Mexican artillery and infantry and three field pieces in position, behind a low parapet. This position could at the time have been taken with but little trouble or loss, and I so reported it to General Twiggs on my return that afternoon.

In the meantime, Lieutenant Tower with Generals Pillow and Shields [14] with their staffs, had also reconnoitered the ground in front of the enemy's line of works and selected points of attack.

On the evening of the 13th General Patterson being still sick in bed with a most violent attack of fever which at first came upon him whilst in Vera Cruz—General Twiggs made all the arrangements for an assault of the enemy's positions early the next morning, about day-break. He ordered that Pillow and Shields should attack the works which they had that day reconnoitered, whilst he would attack with his own division the position of Cerro Gordo, and having taken it, would then, if necessary take in rear the works which Pillow and Shields were to attack in front.

After all the officers had received their instructions and left

---

[14] General Gideon J. Pillow, President James K. Polk's law partner, commanded first a brigade and later a division in the army; General James Shields was a brigade commander under Twiggs and John A. Quitman.

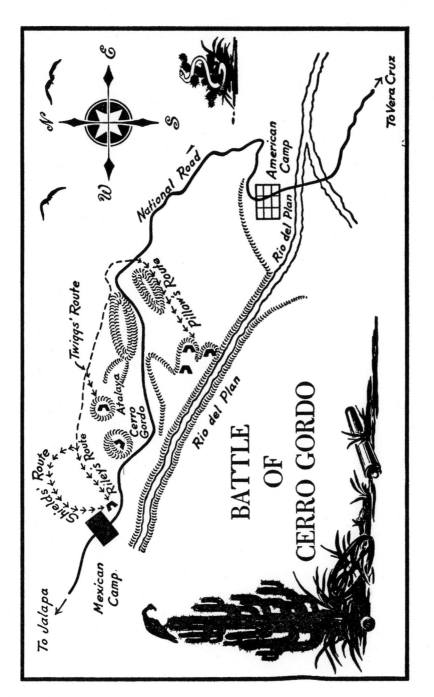

BATTLE
OF
CERRO GORDO

To Jalapa

Mexican Camp.

Shield's Route

Riley's Route

Twiggs' Route

Atalaya

Cerro Gordo

Rio del Plan

Pillow's Route

National Road

American Camp

Rio del Plan

To Vera Cruz

General Twiggs's quarters, I repaired to my own at General Patterson's division to make my arrangements for the next morning's operations, for upon me had devolved the duty of leading Twiggs's division. General Patterson sent for me to know the result of my reconnoissance and he made some enquiries relative to the intended attack. In the course of the conversation, he asked me if I felt confident of success, and if, in my opinion, the plan adopted was the best that could have been devised.

I replied to him, in presence of his aide, Lieutenant Colonel Abercrombie,[15] and I believe also his other aide, Lieutenant Williams,[16] that I thought we would undoubtedly succeed, but that I would have preferred a different plan of attack. That the enemy being about twice as numerous as we were (13 or 14,000 men) and occupying a very long line of strong position, I thought it was not the best plan to divide our already too weak forces to attack him on his two flanks at once; when, from the rough and broken nature of the country we had to operate upon, the two attacks could have no relation with each other, whilst the failure at one point might jeopardize the result at the other; for the enemy occupying a central position to our lines of operations, might then concentrate all his means in not only grasping the victory from our hands, but even in endangering our retreat in case it should become necessary to make one. That I thought, the better plan would be to concentrate all our disposable means on the key of all those positions, the Cerro Gordo hill, so as to take it at once, and then take the others in rear! That however, a demonstration might be made with either Pillow's or Shields' brigade, in front of the enemy's front line of works, to keep in position the forces there, and

[15] John J. Abercrombie.

[16] This is probably Lieutenant Thomas Williams, later a staff officer with Scott.

to prevent them from making a descent upon our encampment.

After listening attentively to all I had to say, General Patterson then suggested that it might perhaps be well for me to go back to General Twiggs and explain my views to him. After hesitating a while at the responsibility I was about to assume, especially as I was without much practical experience in such matters and almost unacquainted with General Twiggs, I left him, asking Colonel Abercrombie to accompany me, to support my views if necessary, and to be a witness to the interview.

We found General Twiggs alone, I believe, or with his aides (Lieutenants Brooks and McDonald) [17] constantly coming in and going out, to see to the transmission of his orders. I then asked him, hesitatingly, if he would permit me to make a few remarks relative to his plan of attack? He replied immediately and kindly, "Certainly, Sir, and I will be happy to listen to you." I then told him in pretty nearly the same terms, all that I had said to General Patterson, without stating however that I had said anything to the latter on the subject—for I knew the dislike which existed between them and I did not wish him to suppose that General Patterson wanted to interfere in his arrangements. After pausing and reflecting a while, he said to me, "You may be right, Sir, but it is already late (it was already night), I have given all my orders, and to change them now, might occasion too much confusion and uncertainty. Don't you think we will succeed anyhow?" I told him, "Certainly, Sir, but I think we ought to throw all the chances in our favor."

About this time or a little later in the evening, General Patterson having heard that General Scott would arrive the next day, countermanded the whole attack! I still think, had it taken place, that General Twiggs with his known penetration and quick decision, would have altered his original plan of

[17] Philip W. McDonald.

attack by the next morning, before reaching the field of battle, which was nearly three miles from our encampment at Plan del Rio.

General Scott arrived there at 2 h. p. m. on the 14th and immediately commenced collecting all the information which we had in our possession and which I had laid down on my sketch, which was submitted to him.

On the 15th I went with Captain Lee and some other Engineer officers to examine again the same path. When we arrived at the foot of the Atalaya they ascended to its crest and I went around its base to the foot of the Cerro Gordo, about one-half mile farther than on the 13th, as Colonel Sumner [18] and the officers of the Rifle Regiment which I had as an escort this time, can testify to if required. In the afternoon of that day having another attack of the fever which I had taken in Vera Cruz, I was compelled to return to Plan del Rio, marking, however, with a hatchet as I went along, the road which was afterwards made on the 17th. At 8 h. a. m. on the 18th, the attack commenced, and I reported to Major Smith [19] for duty, although still suffering from the fever—in consequence of which, I was assigned to duty with the General Staff instead of being attached to one of the attacking columns—for I could then hardly support myself in my saddle.

On the 16th and 17th Captain Lee carried my reconnoissance about one-half a mile farther, but it cannot be denied that on the 15th, we knew nearly all that was ascertained afterwards, and that a good deal of precious time was lost in reconnoitering, whilst the enemy's strength and number was increasing every hour; whereas ours had attained its maximum when Worth's division joined us on the evening of the 18th. It was

[18] E. V. Sumner, Second Dragoons, who later was a Federal corps commander in the Army of the Potomac.

[19] John L. Smith, of the Engineer Company.

also a loss of time and labor to put those two 24-pounders on the crest of the Atalaya hill—they did more noise than execution. To attack an enemy's position or line of battle, especially when during every hour he is adding to his strength, in obstacles, artillery and number, only a most rapid and close reconnoissance is needed; then the General in Chief should watch the chances for striking the decisive blow on the strategic point in the critical moment as the battle progresses, as was done at Churubusco by the General in Chief, and at Contreras by General Smith.[20] I consider it unnecessary to enter into the details of the battle of Cerro Gordo as the description given of it by Ripley is sufficiently accurate and minute.[21]

Immediately after the battle and whilst transmitting an order, I came suddenly upon a group of our sapper-company surrounding a wounded officer along the main road. I immediately thought it might possibly be one of the gallant Engineers attached to said Company; but upon enquiring I found it was a Mexican Colonel (Martines), aid to General Pincón,[22] second in command, who had been nearly cut in two by a cannon ball! He requested me in good French to send him one of our surgeons as soon as practicable, for he was then suffering beyond all description! I promised to do so, at the same time ordering him to be conveyed to our ambulance, but whether he ever reached it is more than doubtful—for I did not suppose he had much longer to suffer in this world. He was quite a fine looking and intelligent young man. Peace be to his ashes! if dead, he died a noble death.

[20] The General in Chief referred to here and many times later is, of course, Scott. General Persifor F. Smith commanded a brigade in Twiggs's division. See note 32 below.

[21] Beauregard is citing the two-volume work by R. S. Ripley, *War with Mexico* (New York, 1849).

[22] This is probably Louis Pinzón.

Beauregard in Mexico

At Santa Anna's [23] *hacienda* of the Encero, nine miles in the rear of Cerro Gordo which he had left only that morning, we found (Lee and myself) a large quantity of maps, drawings, of works, captured letters from the families of our officers, etc., and after a careful sifting of them all, we took possession of the most important of the first, and transmitted the latter to those to whom they were addressed.

[23] Antonio López de Santa Anna, President of Mexico and commander of its armies. One of Mexico's most flamboyant military politicians, Santa Anna was living in exile in Cuba when the war started. The United States Department of State spirited him into Mexico in the hope that he would take over the government and conclude a favorable peace treaty. Upon his arrival he announced that he had made his way through the American naval blockade at great peril in order to lead the defense of his country against the invaders.

Santa Anna was a man of great ability and driving determination. Had it not been for him, the Mexicans probably would have capitulated sooner. As a general, he showed great skill, but he tended to overlook important details. He owned several *haciendas* or large estates.

The Approaches to Mexico City

AUGUST 7–15, 1847

ON the 7th of August the army, divided into four divisions, Twiggs's, Quitman's,[24] Worth's, and Pillow's left Puebla on successive days on its way to the City of Mexico, all the Engineer officers being attached to headquarters. We reached Ayotla at 3 h. P. M. on the 11th, and on the morning of the 12th, Captains Lee and Mason and Lieutenant Stevens,[25] went to reconnoiter El Penon only eight or nine miles from Ayotla,

[24] John A. Quitman. Of Scott's general officers, Pillow, Quitman, Shields, Pierce, and Cadwalader came from civilian life. Patterson was a civilian but had had long experience in the Pennsylvania militia. P. F. Smith had been a lawyer and militia officer; he remained in the army after the war. In fine, most of Scott's principal officers were amateurs. Only Worth and Twiggs were professionals.

[25] James L. Mason and Isaac I. Stevens.

Major Smith, myself, and Lieutenant Tower, going to the top of the Calderon hill in front of El Penon, to take a general view of the Valley of Mexico. In the afternoon of the same day Captain Lee and myself reconnoitered the northern shore of Lake Chalco to a small village (San Francisco) situated near the causeway separating said lake from the one called Xochimilco, and obtained there some information relative to the road on the other side of these lakes, which was reported as quite good, although narrow and rough, but corroborating in this the information which had been obtained in Puebla, when preparing the maps for the movements of the Army, from those of Baron Humbolt.[26]

On the morning of the 13th Captain Mason, Lieutenant McClellan and myself escorted by one company of Dragoons and the Rifle Regiment went out to reconnoiter in front and about Mexicalcingo, passing in front of El Penon, where we left General Smith's brigade in observation with Lieutenant Stevens to complete the reconnoissance at that point. Captain Lee and Lieutenant Tower following the road along Lake Chalco which we had reconnoitered on the evening of the 11th, came to meet us in front of Mexicalcingo, where we had arrived at about noon. On our way thither, Captain Canby (Riley's assistant adjutant general),[27] Lieutenant McClellan and myself and two or three dragoons, while extending our reconnoissance in rear of what is called from its shape and appearance the *Star-hill,* came suddenly upon a party of some twenty-five Lancers, well equipped and caparisoned; we immediately charged upon them at great speed, but before we had reached

[26] Alexander von Humboldt was a German scientist who is regarded as one of the fathers of modern geography. He had written extensively on his travels in Mexico.

[27] E. R. S. Canby, later a Union general; Colonel Bennet Riley was a brigade commander under Twiggs.

them, they turned about and by hard spurring and yelling, managed to get across a *barranca* or ravine and to reach a small village near by, which saved them from being captured. When they had got out of our reach, however, they turned around and opened upon us with their *escopetas* [muskets], but fortunately without effect; and as the main column of our escort was several miles from us, we thought it prudent not to pursue them any farther.

We found the position of Mexicalcingo naturally a strong one and pretty well fortified, but with few guns in position and a small force to defend it. It was generally thought, that if immediately, properly and boldly attacked, it could have been taken without much loss—for it was isolated, had no direct communication with Santa Anna's army, all collected at El Penon and from which it could not have derived timely assistance, especially if a strong demonstration had in the meantime been kept up in front of El Penon; to maintain Santa Anna in position, until it was too late for him to get to Mexicalcingo by the way of the City of Mexico. Whereas if he had followed in our rear, we could not have adopted a better plan to draw him out in the open field, and the fate of himself and army would soon have been decided, for then only one regiment and two pieces of artillery could have kept at bay the force defending Mexicalcingo! At any rate, the attack on Mexicalcingo, although similar in some respects to that on "Arcola" by Napoleon, would not by any means have presented the same difficulties.

On our return to Ayotla, Captain Canby having ventured alone, rather too far from our escort, was suddenly attacked by a few mounted *peones* provided with their long lassos and before he could get at his pistols, they were so near to him that he had in all haste to put spurs to his horse, but not before, however, one of them had thrown his lasso at him, fortunately only catching his hat! Which remained in their possession and was

43

afterwards paraded about the streets of Mexico in great triumph, with Lieutenant McClellan's spy-glass, which he had lost in our pursuit of the Mexican Lancers.

We arrived at Ayotla a little before dark and reported the result of our reconnoissance to the General in Chief—who immediately commenced making the necessary preparations for an attack in that direction in case the reconnoissance to be made around the south of Lake Chalco did not corroborate the reports which we had obtained both at Puebla and about Ayotla, as to the nature and condition of the roads in that direction.

This reconnoissance should have been made by the Engineer officers on the 11th, 12th, or 13th, but on the latter day General Worth whose headquarters were at Chalco, having proposed, or offered, to have it done by Colonel Duncan,[28] who had volunteered for that duty, and the General in Chief only waiting for a *responsible person* to say that this road was good and practicable, and supposing that his Engineer officers had at that time as much as they could well attend to, wishing moreover to have the matter investigated as soon as possible—readily acceded to Worth's proposition, and thus this reconnoissance was made by Colonel Duncan on the morning of the 14th, Worth having obtained said permission before our return from Mexicalcingo. But I have it from Colonel Duncan himself, that he only went as far as Tuliahualco, nearly opposite to where Lee and myself had gone (at San Francisco) on the evening of the 11th, which village (Tuliahualco) is only eight or nine miles from Chalco—and about 12 miles from San Augustin [San Agustin]—and from this reconnoissance he made his report on the whole route! confirming, however, again, what Lee and myself had heard also at San Francisco; and for this reconnoissance of nine miles, he had an escort of nearly 1,000 men. Finding the roads good that far, and hearing that they were

[28] James Duncan, Worth's artillery chief.

44

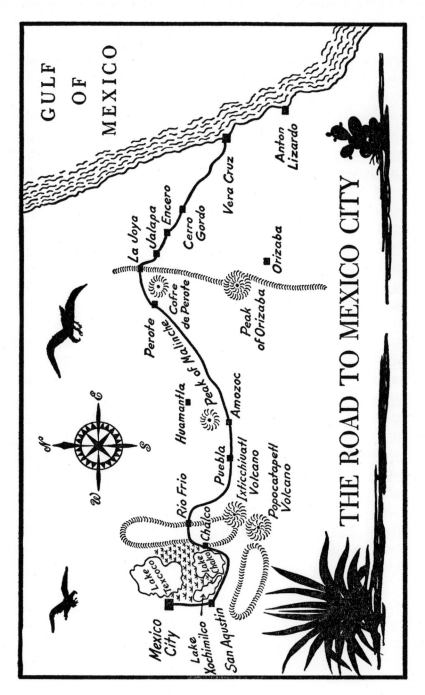

GULF OF MEXICO

Anton Lizardo

Vera Cruz

Cerro Gordo

Encero

Jalapa

La Joya

Orizaba

Cofre de Perote

Peak of Orizaba

Perote

Peak of Malinche

Huamantla

Amozoc

Puebla

Ixticchivatl Volcano

Popocatapetl Volcano

Rio Frio

Chalco

Lake Texcoco

Lake Chalco

Mexico City

Lake Xochimilco

San Agustin

THE ROAD TO MEXICO CITY

45

as good, if not better, further on, he returned to Chalco at about 2 h. P. M. that day, and immediately went to Ayotla to make his report to the General in Chief.

I am far from wishing to detract from the merits of Colonel Duncan; his reputation belongs to the country and to the whole army, and he certainly was considered one of the best and most efficient of our younger officers, but his friends ought to rest satisfied with what he really did to win his fame, and ought not to endeavor to *tack on* to him credit which did not properly belong to him. He did nothing more on this occasion than what was constantly being done by all the Engineer officers and it is a public and indisputable fact, that the General in Chief never on a single occasion, gave an order for an attack or an important movement when near the enemy, without first having received the reports of all his Engineer officers, for it was only after having received said reports that he made up his mind *finally*—and if still, doubts existed, he then went to examine for himself; I never, on a single occasion, saw him go to what was not the decisive point or position. His judgment and *"coup d'oeil"* were always unquestionably correct on such occasions.

On the morning of the 14th Mason and myself received orders to report to General Worth at Chalco for duty—where we arrived at about noon, and at about 2 h. P. M. Colonel Duncan returned from his reconnoissance. He immediately repaired to headquarters at Ayotla, where the General in Chief was awaiting his return before issuing his final orders, for the movement towards Mexicalcingo or Chalco.

The Battle of Contreras
AUGUST 15–20, 1847

ON the afternoon of the 15th, we commenced the march to San Agustin, where we arrived without much difficulty or opposition from the enemy, at about 2 h. P. M. on the 17th. On the morning of the 18th, Major Smith, Mason, Stevens and Tower, went to reconnoiter the works of San Antonio on the direct road to the City of Mexico, which is about nine from San Agustin. Lee and myself with an escort of one battalion and two companies of dragoons went to reconnoiter those at Contreras, about five miles to the North-west, in front of which we met a strong *piquet* or advanced guard of the enemy, which we attacked and dispersed, killing, wounding and taking about one dozen of them. We found the road pretty good for about

47

half the distance, but the rest was quite rough, hilly and partly covered with *pedregal,* but saw it could be made practicable (with a little trouble and labor) for artillery.

The enemy's works, however, commanded that portion of it across the *pedregal* [lava field] which was nearest to them, but at this point, as a matter of course, the battle would have to be fought; it was true, over rough ground, but only against one of Santa Anna's divisions, and as we felt confident we could defeat the whole army, the result in our minds could not have been doubtful one moment, and it surely would have been decided at once, had General Scott arrived on the ground three or four hours sooner on the 19th—for on that day we commenced the construction of the road at about 9 h. and by 1 h. had got it to within reach of the enemy's guns, and instead of halting here for further orders, under the pretence of protecting the working parties (which could not have proceeded any further, whilst exposed to a powerful battery of twenty-two guns) an action was commenced which by dark looked so desperate that no one could *father it.* It was most of the time (until the arrival of the General in Chief) confusion worse confounded, every one seeming to be *on his own hook*—orders and counter-orders succeeding each other with increased rapidity as the crisis seemed to approach, until we got beyond their reach on the other side of the *pedregal!* When General Scott reached the field of battle at about 3 or 4 h. he beheld with dismay his forces in the d——dest *scatteration* that perhaps he or any other general ever saw before, unless in a defeat; being hardly able to communicate with them on account of the infernal *pedregal* which separated him from them.

After the construction of that road had been discontinued as already stated, I made several attempts to get Major Smith's consent in allowing me to accompany some of the forces which were moving across the *pedregal* towards the village of San

48

Geronimo, but did not succeed until Colonel Morgan's [29] regiment, the Fifteenth Infantry, having lost its way in the *pedregal,* whilst moving to the support of Cadwalader [30] stumbled upon us; I then obtained permission to pilot it to its destination, with orders, however, to return immediately. We reached Cadwalader's position near the above village at about 5 h. and found that Santa Anna had already collected immediately in his front, at the distance of about 1,000 yards an army of nearly 8,000 men with two pieces of artillery—presenting a most imposing and beautiful appearance. In his rear at about the same distance, Cadwalader had the fortified position of Contreras defended by Valencia,[31] with twenty-two pieces of artillery and about 5 or 8,000 men, without his knowing exactly the position of Smith's or Riley's brigade, the latter of which he had sent to support.

I reported to him the arrival of Morgan's regiment, and told him that my orders being to return immediately, I would do so as soon as I had rested awhile, and would bear any message to the General in Chief, which he might wish to communicate to him. He told me to inform him of the critical position which he occupied and to tell him to send him reinforcements as soon as it could be done, for Santa Anna would evidently attack him shortly. I hesitated awhile whether I would not offer him my services as an Engineer officer, notwithstanding Major Smith's orders, but he did not appear to want them or at any rate to suppose that I could be of any use to him—so after resting five or ten minutes, I started on my painful and fatiguing trip across the *pedregal.*

[29] George W. Morgan.

[30] General George Cadwalader was a brigade commander in Pillow's division.

[31] General Gabriel Valencia commanded the Mexican forces around Contreras.

Beauregard in Mexico

As I came to the ravine passing at the foot of Contreras and which separated me from the *pedregal* I was about to enter; whilst looking for a favorable place to ford the little stream at the bottom of it, I heard some one call me by name on the other side of it, and looking up had the pleasure of beholding General Smith,[32] who was about to cross to my side. He succeeded in doing so and asked me for the news and on what duty I was then employed. I told him what I had seen and the message I was then carrying to the General in Chief—adding at the same time that I would gladly remain with him if he would give me the order; for I disliked exceedingly the idea of recrossing that *pedregal,* my shoes and pantaloons being already very badly torn. He immediately gave me the order, at the same time saying that his brigade being near by, he supposed that would be reinforcement enough.

He then told me to take him to Cadwalader, whom we found near where I had just left him. His countenance immediately brightened up, when he saw us, and he said to General Smith,—"I suppose, Sir, you assume the command here?" "Certainly, with pleasure," replied Smith, and having heard all that he had to communicate to him, he said to me, "Let us look at our position, and at that fellow's, Santa Anna, whilst my brigade is coming up." We commenced making our ex-

[32] Persifor F. Smith was a brigade commander under Twiggs and one of the best officers in the army. Born in Philadelphia in 1798, he moved to New Orleans in 1819 and started the practice of law. He rose rapidly in his profession, and also became adjutant general of the Louisiana militia. Although Beauregard's narrative does not indicate the fact, it is highly probable that he knew Smith before the war. Whatever the case, Smith, as a result of his contacts with Beauregard in this and in other battles, came to have a great admiration for the young engineer officer. His friendship was important. A skilled soldier and a magnetic leader, Smith remained in the army after the war, becoming one of its most trusted leaders. He died in 1858 while serving in Utah Territory.

amination during the course of which we stumbled upon Lee, who had also just arrived *on his own hook,* and we continued together our reconnoissance. When the General's brigade had arrived, he placed it in position principally in the village and to the left of Cadwalader's.

In the meantime nothing definite was known of Riley's position; it was known that he was not far from us, but where no one could tell exactly—and there was even at a time a rumor that he was killed: which cast quite a gloom over us all, for he was known to be a *host in himself* whenever the fighting would commence. Santa Anna's bands in our front were all this while playing lustily magnificent marches and other martial airs and we could see him distinctly moving about with his immense staff, from one end of his line to the other. Every now and then his two pieces of artillery would send us their deadly messengers, but after awhile it became apparent that he was not going to attack us that evening, why we could not tell; but I strongly suspected on account of the difficulties of the ground between us—which appeared to me to be cut up with ravines and *barrancas* [gorges]; how deep and how large I could not tell.

A little before dark, Riley, to our extreme joy, made his appearance at the head of his brigade, and Smith made up his mind to get rid of Santa Anna before night, by attacking him at once. He in consequence ordered Lee and myself to examine a pretty large ravine which was at the foot of our position to see if it were easily passable, and he ordered Riley and Cadwalader to form their brigades in close columns of divisions at half distance, left in front, the first to attack the right of Santa Anna's line and the latter the middle, his own brigade to act with Riley's and as circumstances might dictate.

This attack however, I, for one, was far from approving, notwithstanding my confidence in, and admiration of, General Smith's judgment and military capacity, in which respect he likely stood second (in the opinion of the army generally) only to the General in Chief. I endeavored to get Captain Lee, Lieutenant Colonel Johnston,[33] of the Voltigeurs, and others, to advise the General otherwise; for, as a matter of course, I dared not say anything on the subject, on account of my subordinate rank and position—but these officers, either not coinciding with me in opinion, or thinking the interference might not be well received, refused to have anything to do with it. Fortunately (as I think) before Cadwalader's column of new troops could be formed, it became so dark that the attack had to be given up—Riley's and Smith's [troops] being, however, ready in about ten minutes.

My reasons for objecting to it were these:

1st. We could not clearly discover the nature of the ground which separated us from the enemy's postion—and which I thought was cut up with deep gullies or ravines, running nearly parallel to our line of battle (as it proved to be the case afterwards).

2nd. Before we could have reached the enemy, it would have been quite dark, and by the time the fighting would have been fairly under way, it would have been impossible to distinguish friends from foes.

3rd. Cadwalader's brigade which was to have attacked the middle of the enemy's line, consequently the strongest part of it, was composed entirely of new levies who had never been before under fire.

---

[33] Joseph E. Johnston. See note 10. In the Civil War, Johnston was one of the Confederacy's ranking generals. He and Beauregard were intimately associated during the conflict. They shared the command at the first battle of Manassas, and Beauregard served under Johnston in 1861–62 and in the closing months of the war. Firm military comrades, they quarreled bitterly in the postwar period when they wrote their war reminiscences.

The Battle of Contreras

4th. The moment the movement would have commenced and we could have been seen on the rising ground in our front by Valencia at Contreras, he would necessarily have opened a terrible fire of heavy artillery upon our rear, which would alone have disconcerted the whole attack.

5th and lastly. It was risking the fate of the whole campaign in a movement the favorable issue of which was not commensurate with the odds against us—and moreover if made at all, it should have been made on the left of Santa Anna's line (his right resting on a deep ravine running towards us) to cut him off from his base of operations at San Angel and Churubusco, especially as his two pieces of artillery being on the left of that line would otherwise have taken our columns in flank. I considered that we had only two things to do: either to recross the *pedregal* during the night, as did Lee, and rejoin our base of operations; or *whip* Valencia out of his fort, take it and thereby re-open our communications with General Scott —but the latter attack as a matter of course, could not be attempted until morning.

Of course, I did not enter into all these reasons with the officers above cited, for we then had hardly time to act; much less to talk or discuss; but whilst in the church that night, I spoke freely on the subject to the officers then present of whom I recollect now Lieutenant G. W. Smith (and McClellan I believe) and Dr. Cuyler;[34] remarking at the time to them, that I was sorry we had not told Lee to have several bright lights kept up during the night on the hill where we had left the General's headquarters, to direct us in our march across the *pedregal* in case anything turned up, to prevent the attack on Contreras (which by that time had been determined upon).

[34] Surgeon John M. Cuyler. Beauregard and other officers were spending the night in the church at San Geronimo, which is the village referred to in the next paragraph.

Beauregard in Mexico

A short time after having given up the attack on Santa Anna, it commenced raining heavily (which by the by would only have added to the obstacles we would have had to contend with) but just about then, General Smith was informed that Lieutenants Tower, Brooks, and Canby (the last two of Twiggs's and Riley's staffs) had reconnoitered a ravine starting from a village we occupied, going to the rear of the position of Contreras, and by which it could be approached very closely without being perceived. Smith then said, "If that be the case, we will attack it before daylight," at which we were all delighted. Those young officers having confirmed that report, he immediately gave his orders accordingly, sending Lee to inform the General in Chief of the movement. That night Lieutenants Tower and Brooks again reconnoitered the ravine and found it knee deep with water from the rain which was then falling in torrents.

The troops slept under arms as well as they could, and the staff with the wounded took refuge in the church of the village, a large and massive stone building—where at about 11 h. P. M. General Shields reported and received his orders from General Smith, neither at the time suspecting that the former was the ranking officer. At about 3 h. A. M. on the 20th the rain still falling we took up our line of march to surprise Valencia, and after wading knee-deep in mud and water, we arrived unperceived, just about daybreak within 500 yards in the rear of his position. We then halted awhile to close up our columns and dry our arms.

In the meantime a rapid reconnoissance was made by General Smith and his general staff. Riley then moved to the attack and I was directed to put the Rifle Regiment in position, supported by one regiment of infantry, along a ravine which advanced quite close up to the work, and from which a very effective fire could be kept on the enemy's gunners and infantry, thickly gathered inside of the fort. In the performance of which duty I was greatly assisted by Lieutenants Smith and McClellan of the Engineers, and their behavior as well as that of their sapper-company cannot be too highly praised. That infantry regiment did not however, support the Rifles, which event was unfortunate; for had it done so, I could have cut off the retreat of the enemy at the bridge, as Lieutenant Colonel Hébert [35] will testify, for I sent to him at the critical moment, but his colonel would not consent to his coming where I was with the Rifles, saying that he had no orders to that affect.

The attack commenced at about 5½ h. A. M. and resulted in a most complete victory in less than 20 minutes, as timed by General Smith himself. I was then sent by him to inform General Scott of our brilliant success. It was about 6½ h. before I could get a horse for that purpose, and when I came to the bridge near the works, I there met with General Twiggs who enquired for the news and appeared delighted on hearing them. After crossing the ravine at the foot of the fort and about 400 yards from said ravine, I met General Pillow accompanied by one of his aides; the latter stopped to ask the news also, but the former only spurred on his horse the faster.

I then continued across the *pedregal*, saw the "debris" of Magruder's [36] battery, and had got about half way to San Agustin de las Cueras, near a paper factory belonging to an Englishman (Mr. Benfield, I believe) when I met Generals Scott and Worth with their staffs. They were still ignorant of the result of our attack, and when I told them of it, three cheers were given for our brilliant success. General Scott then said to

[35] Paul O. Hébert, Eleventh Infantry.

[36] Captain John Bankhead Magruder, light artillery. His battery was under heavy fire during the battle. Magruder became a Confederate general, serving in Virginia and Texas. He never fulfilled the brilliant promise of his Mexican War career.

me, "Young man, if I were not on horseback, I would embrace
you," and he then added, turning around to those about him,
"Gentlemen, if West Point had only produced the Corps of
Engineers, the Country ought to be proud of that institution":
thus repaying us amply, in a few words, for all our toils and
dangers!

Worth then asked him, whether he could not commence his
movement against San Antonio? And I am under the impression that he replied to him, "Yes, sir, but cautiously until you
hear firing about the enemy's rear."

We then rode to Contreras and I received orders with Lieutenant Tower to remain there, to repair the road across the
pedregal and the deep ravine at the foot of the work, with the
prisoners taken that morning, who would be ordered to report
to us for that duty; our artillery and wagons would then pass
in that direction, on their way to San Angel.

I remained there for some time waiting for those prisoners
and assisting those trains across said ravine as well as I could
with the few men I had about me. After a while, hearing some
firing in the direction of San Angel or Churubusco, and Lieutenant Tower not having reported to me, I concluded that
another battle was about to be fought in that direction, and I
started off to take a part in it; but having gone about half way,
I reflected that the first duty of the soldier was to obey orders,
that all the Engineer officers were with the army and that I
had been ordered to perform a secondary duty at present; it
was true, but which might become a very important one for
the future movements of the army, and that if through my dis-
obedience it was not performed my commission would certainly be forfeited.

So I turned back again towards Contreras, and when I
arrived there, I found that the prisoners having received no

orders to report to me, had been marched to San Agustin. I immediately started after them, and when I got there, I was informed that the enemy having been driven from San Antonio, and the road in that direction being in a much better condition, the trains had been ordered to move by it instead of by the one which passed near Contreras. I then started to join the General's staff, which I met on the way, just returning from Churubusco that had been fought in the meantime. Of course, I was much disappointed and chagrined, but myself and horse being pretty well worn out with fatigue, I returned to my quarters at San Agustin, where I took my first meal since my breakfast the day before! during that time having only eaten a few pieces of hard bread given to me by some of the sappers.

I will here add, that at the assault on Contreras, I had the satisfaction to receive the swords of Colonel Reyes,[37] Chief Engineer, and Colonel ———, Chief of the Artillery to General Valencia, the latter Colonel being seriously wounded in the shoulder.

During the pursuit we came to a large stone building along the road surrounded by a high wall. It seemed to be crowded by Mexicans, some of whom were holding white handkerchiefs out of the windows. I immediately went in that direction, and entered into the yard of the building. I found a great many of our soldiers talking with the Mexicans, but unable to understand each other. Finding all the lower doors and windows strongly barricaded, I asked to open one of them that I might go in and speak to their commanding officer, but they refused saying that they were afraid of our soldiers. They at the same time told me that General Salas,[38] the second in command to General Valencia, was in the building with them. The reason

[37] I. Reyes.
[38] José Mariano Salas.

57

of their excess of precaution was now explained to me; for this Salas, the ex-Acting President of the Republic, was reputed for his violent passions and ardent patriotism, and he had but a few weeks before published an address to his countrymen, exhorting them "to prosecute against the infamous yankees a war of extermination, a war to the knife, granting or accepting no quarter." He was now fearful we might be guided towards him by his own infamous principles.

I told them that belonging to General Smith's staff, I wanted to get into the building to speak to General Salas. They then directed me to another part of the edifice, by the side of which stood the ruins of an old wall from which I could get in through one of the rear windows. I did so, and soon found myself in the midst of such a confused crowd as I had never been into before. Officers and men, the wounded and the dying, all herded together in one mass of confusion and fear. I however found in the midst of them a young officer who spoke French quite well, and who piloted me to the room where General Salas was walking to and fro in apparently quite a nervous state of mind, with a nervous twitch about the mouth, but with a quick and piercing grey or black eye, and withal an expression of decision and firmness about his whole person, which denoted he had made up his mind for the worst.

He seemed to be about fifty-five years of age, rather spare and below the middle stature; I went up to him hesitating whether I would not take his sword from him, but finally concluded that perhaps he was to a certain extent excusable as his motive was certainly a worthy one, the defense of his country! So I merely told him, through the Mexican officer, that General Smith would soon be there to receive him as a prisoner of war and that he had nothing to fear, for, we, Americans, gloried ourselves, not only in sparing the lives of our prisoners, but also in affording them ample protection! He appeared relieved

58

at my words, but did not seem very thankful for my remarks. He replied that he hoped to see General Smith soon, as they were very crowded where they were. I then left him and very soon after having met with General Smith, I told him *the kind of a bird he had in his cage.*

Reconnaissances before Mexico City
SEPTEMBER 6–11, 1847

DURING the armistice no reconnoissance was permitted by the General in Chief, although it was a notorious fact, that the enemy was violating it day and night.

On the evening of the 7th of September I was ordered to make, at Pillow's suggestion, a *night reconnoissance* in front of the Southern gates of the City of Mexico—about the San Antonio or Nino-perdido roads (over a section of country which *I had never seen before*) and if possible to penetrate into the city itself. I endeavored to object to it, stating that such a reconnoissance was never employed except on ground already well known, and to ascertain a particular fact which could not be got at in daytime or in any other way—such as the practicability of a breach—the passage of a ditch, etc., but General Pillow being anxious to have it done, and General Scott being solicitous to please him—I was to be the *"Trait d'union"* between the two —in other words the *victim* very likely for this uncalled for expedition.

I started at about 1 h. A. M. on the 8th from the *hacienda Nalvarte,* with a Mexican guide furnished me by General Pillow and an escort of four companies commanded by Captain Casey [39] of Riley's brigade. We took the Nino-perdido road and advanced quietly until we came to near its intersection with the Piedad Crossroad; here seeing the road much darkened by the overhanging trees on each side of it, and learning from the guide, who appeared much frightened, that we were not far from one of the gates of the city, I concluded that the enemy had probably a *piquet* at that point and I in consequence halted the column, and took a platoon with me in advance, with orders as soon as we were hailed by the sentinel to rush upon him and take him, without however firing under any consideration; for the enemy's batteries which were not far off, would then probably open upon us; the same advice was given to the main escort, which was to follow me some distance in the rear.

I then started on with my platoon and the guide by my side, whom I ordered as soon as we were challenged to answer in Spanish. After advancing about one hundred paces, I saw a white object [a Mexican soldier] suddenly appear in the middle of the road, about seventy-five yards from us, and after listening to us awhile—he cried out in aloud voice, *"Quién vive?"* I took hold of the guide to tell him to answer—but he was so frightened that he could not! The cry was again repeated, and finding that my guide was trembling like a leaf, I replied, assuming the Spanish accent as well as I could, *"Amigos!"* and then turning to my platoon, I told them, "Now, men, let

[39] Silas Casey, later a Union general.

us rush upon him"; but I had hardly said so, when, having cocked his gun at his second summons, he levelled it and fired upon us. Immediately a strong *piquet* near by, rushed to his assistance and opened a tremendous fire which threw my platoon (unfortunately composed of recruits from Captain C. Ridgeley's company) into great confusion! My guide in the meantime, jumped into the canal along side of the road, where I supposed he had got drowned.

I turned around and had the satisfaction at any rate to apply to my platoon those words of Caesar to his legions in Spain when in the same condition that my platoon was in at that time, "Where are you going to, you are mistaken, the enemy is here and not there!" The main escort however soon came to the rescue, and we charged on the *piquet* which knew better than to wait for us. The alarm however was immediately given at the *garitas* in front of the city, and signals were made to show that they were ready to receive us, and having moreover lost my guide (who had returned to the *hacienda Nalvarte* where we found him on our return at 3 h. A. M.), this put an end to my night reconnoissance, which could only have resulted in failure or disaster, as I had foreseen.

About daybreak, as we were about to start for the same spot again on a *day reconnoissance,* we received orders to hold ourselves in readiness to march to Worth's assistance at Molino del Rey, if needed—and an hour or two afterwards we started from the *hacienda Nalvarte* for that purpose; but arrived too late to take a part in that unfortunate and bloody battle. Mason and Foster were Worth's Engineer officers and they were both severely wounded. When the order came to Major Smith, on the evening of the 7th, to detail an officer to assist Mason, as I was quite friendly with him, I offered my services for that duty, but as luck would have it, the Major ordered Foster to report to him. Not five minutes afterwards another order came to detail

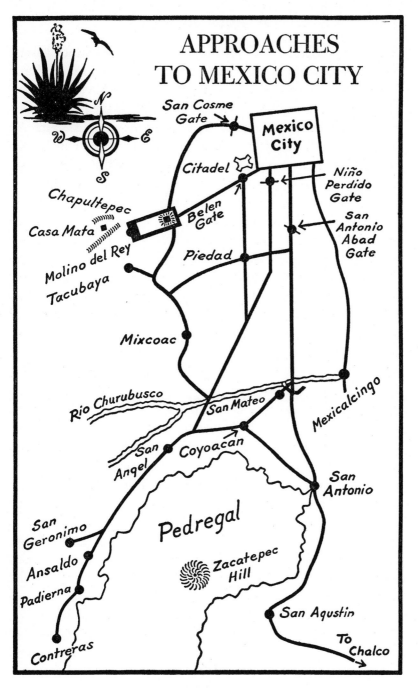

APPROACHES TO MEXICO CITY

San Cosme Gate

Mexico City

Citadel

Niño Perdido Gate

Belen Gate

San Antonio Abad Gate

Chapultepec

Casa Mata

Molino del Rey

Tacubaya

Piedad

Mixcoac

Rio Churubusco

San Mateo

Mexicalcingo

San Angel

Coyoacan

San Antonio

San Geronimo

Ansaldo

Pedregal

Zacatepec Hill

Padierna

San Agustin

Contreras

To Chalco

an officer to report at headquarters for a night reconnoissance, and I was selected this time, much to my sorrow and regret then, but to my joy afterwards, for I might not then have been able to take a part in the ulterior operations against the city.

The plan of attack against Molino del Rey ought either to have been one of surprise with the bayonet alone, a little before daybreak, or having an abundance of artillery and ammunition at Tacubaya—taken at Contreras and Churubusco, it could all have been used in driving the enemy out of those stone buildings in broad daylight, by merely placing those pieces beyond the range of the guns at Chapultepec; for at the Molino, they had only four light field pieces without a parapet and ditch to protect them! and a sudden charge with the bayonet at double quick time, would then have settled the whole affair in a short while, without the loss of over 100 men! but a sort of mixed attack was adopted which resulted almost in a disaster.

On that same afternoon (the 8th) Lee, Tower and myself returned to the *hacienda Nalvarte* and reconnoitered as far as the village of Piedad. Major Smith and Lieutenant Stevens, not being well enough to undergo much fatigue, remained at headquarters to attend to their duties there. Whenever the circumstances required it however, they were always ready to join us in our more active duties. Lieutenants Smith and McClellan being attached to the Sapper Company, as a matter of course, had little to do generally with our reconnoissance, but had other no less important duites to perform—which to their credit be it said, were always done with the utmost zeal, activity and gallantry. Mason and Foster, as I have already stated, were both severely wounded at the Molinos.

We saw then (Lee, Tower, and myself) that the spot I had reached the night previous, was at about 1,150 yards from the

works at the *garita* of San Antonio, and was then strongly occupied by the enemy! We however advised General Pillow, who
had accompanied us on that reconnoissance, to endeavor to take
possession of it that night, as well as of the village of Piedad,
where we were then, to assist us in making closer reconnoissances hereafter. He accordingly did so.

This *garita* of San Antonio is the one through which a few
(three or four) men from Captain Kearney's [40] command rode,
whilst in pursuit of the enemy after the battle of Churubusco;
only one of them, I believe, escaped with his life, which he
owed to Santa Anna's generosity; for as they were about to
murder him when a prisoner, the former happening to pass
by, ordered him to be released, saying to those around him:
"Gentlemen, if I had many men in my army like this brave
fellow, the yankees would not now be at the gates of Mexico,"
and during the armistice he was sent back to General Scott.
This dragoon was the orderly of General Harney,[41] and just
before the attack on Contreras on the afternoon of the preceding day, he was given my waterproof cloak to hold; he tied
it on the rear of his saddle—as a matter of course, I never saw
it again!

On the 9th the same Engineer officers as above, continued
their reconnoissance in front of the southern gates of the City,
and the enemy was this day concentrated nearer to them.
Riley's brigade and one of Pillow's moved to the village of
Piedad. General Quitman advanced his division from San
Agustin to Coruocan, General Twiggs remaining still at San
Angel with his other brigade (Smith's). Mixcoacue was also

[40] Philip Kearny, First Dragoons. Kearny is the colorful Union general who was killed in the Federal withdrawal after the second battle of
Manassas.

[41] William S. Harney commanded the cavalry and dragoon units.

selected as a general depot for our military stores and our sick. On the 10th Captain Lee went to make some arrangements at the latter place for its future defense, if needed.

Lieutenants Stevens, Tower and myself went to continue the reconnaissances in front of and about the *garita* of San Antonio. Lieutenant Stevens and myself went to within 1,100 yards in front of it, along the main road (Lieutenant Tower going in another direction); and although in full view at the time, we were lucky enough in not being fired at, notwithstanding we could see them distinctly drilling at their pieces at the time—with their commanding officers walking to and fro on the parapets; whenever I saw No. 3 apply their match to their pieces, I would immediately throw myself behind one of the tall poplars which lined the road on each side, till at last, finding that they were merely drilling, I paid no more attention to them and went on to make my sketch of the works at that point, noting the number of pieces in position—the number of embrasures, etc.

After we had got through (in an hour or two) we retraced our steps to rejoin our escort (one regiment of Riley's brigade) which I had left about one mile to our rear, only having taken with us one-half dozen of the best and coolest shots in it. On this occasion we had with us a guide, an American (Mr. Fitzpatrick) who had lived a long time in the City of Mexico as a mail-coach driver to Puebla. He had also been a guide on the 18th of the preceding month to Major Smith and party, when they went to reconnoiter the *hacienda San Antonio,* as already stated. It was on this occasion that the gallant Thornton [42] of the dragoons was killed and the same guide being quite near to him and to an *adobe* house which stood along side of the road,

[42] Captain S. B. Thornton, a dragoon officer. His ambush and capture on the Rio Grande in 1846 had been the pretext of the American declaration of war against Mexico.

the latter was struck by the ball after it had nearly cut Thornton in two, and with the "debris" from the *adobe* house, knocked down several men about it, including the said guide, who was pretty severely bruised, every one thinking at the time that he was killed; but fortunately for him, besides having been pretty badly cut up, he had only lost one of his eyes.

He had in the meantime sufficiently recovered to accompany me on this excursion—but after I had left my escort, I observed that he was becoming more and more fidgety until at last he came up to me and said "Lieutenant, I am perfectly willing to go with you anywhere you please, but if you have not *any particular need of me,* I hope you will remember how badly I have already been treated by that shot which killed Captain Thornton." I told him "Yes, I remember it knocked you into fits, so I fully agree with you and think you had better stay with the escort."

Stevens, Tower and myself returned to headquarters at about sundown, and I having prepared a rough sketch for the General in Chief, we reported "the works quite strong, the ground very unfavorable for the movement of troops, and the enemy quite busy in strengthening the whole line of works on that point." Moreover that day being the anniversary of the taking of Tampico from the Spaniards by Santa Anna himself, we had observed him passing in review at least 15 or 20,000 men in rear of the works at the *garitas* of San Antonio and Mexicalcingo canal! which circumstance very much increased the strength of these works in my own eyes, showing me clearly what to expect when they would be attacked.

The Council at Piedad

SEPTEMBER 11, 1847

ON the morning of the 11th Lieutenant Tower, myself
and Captain Lee, returned to continue the same reconnoissances in another direction however; at about 10 h. we were
informed that the General in Chief had called a meeting of all
the general officers, at the Convent and Church of Piedad, and
that the Engineers were ordered to attend. We immediately
went there and found the meeting already organized. General
Scott commenced by stating "that he had called this meeting
together to have the views of the general officers present as to
the best point by which to attack the City of Mexico! that after
the severe losses we had met with in the several battles of the
Valley already fought, it became a matter of vital importance
to strike a heavy and last blow on that part of the city which

68

offered the greatest probabilities of success with the least chances of loss in officers and men! and that before breaking up this meeting, *he was determined* the orders for the attack should be given, either on one point of the city or on the other."

He then said, "that as he had already reconnoitered the Southern and Western fronts of the city, he would first give them his views as to the one by which the attack ought to be made, but he did not wish them to be influenced in the least by what he was going to say, especially if they had good reasons to differ with him in opinion, for he wanted their views and not his own." He then compared rapidly the advantages and obstacles of the two fronts, and concluded by saying that "in his opinion, the Western gates of the city offered the best chances of success."

General Pillow then got up and after a pretty long speech, which it is useless to enter into, concluded strongly in favor of an attack on the Southern gates of the city. General Quitman then spoke and said, that not having had an opportunity to examine either fronts, having been all this while at San Agustin, he wished to have the views of the Engineer officers. Major Smith, Captain Lee, Lieutenants Stevens and Tower then gave the result of their observations and concluded in favor of an attack on the *Garita* of San Antonio, which opinions decided Generals Quitman, Shields, Cadwalader and Pierce [43] in favor of the same; "notwithstanding the deference" (they said) "which they were disposed to pay to the views and experience of the General in Chief." General Twiggs then said, that not having seen much of either fronts, having been at San Angel all this time, and having only just arrived, he did not expect his opinions could have much weight on either side of the

[43] Franklin Pierce, the future President, commanded a brigade in Pillow's division.

question, but from what he had heard he thought the General in Chief was right in his selection of the point of attack.

General Riley asked the Engineers which front would offer the least time and labor to construct the batteries. He was told the western one. He then replied in his peculiarly blunt way, "Well, I go in for less work and more fighting." Generals Worth and Smith were not present, the first being, at the time, engaged with Captain Huger [44] (ordnance) in selecting the sites of the batteries against Chapultepec (if needed) and the second being on duty at San Angel in charge of the prisoners (I believe) which circumstance by the by, I very much regret, for I should like to have heard his opinion, which I have little doubt, however, would have also coincided with the General in Chief.

In the meantime, Mr. Trist and Colonel Hitchcock [45] were inquiring of me, why I had not given my views? I told them that under no circumstances would I do so, unless called upon personally for them—for differing widely from my brother Engineers, I would be held responsible hereafter in case of non-success for what I would say and consequently would not do so otherwise. I also remembered with a little bitterness, I must confess, the injustice which had been done me in the selection of those batteries at Vera Cruz. Our discussion drew the attention of the General in Chief to that part of the large room where we were, and he then remembered that, although I had been very active in these reconnoissances, I had yet said nothing;

[44] Benjamin Huger, commander of the Ordnance Company, later a Confederate general.

[45] Nicholas P. Trist, chief clerk of the State Department, had been appointed by President Polk as a special agent to accompany the army and, if an opportunity arose, to enter into peace negotiations with the Mexican government. Ethan Allen Hitchcock was Scott's Inspector General; in the Civil War he acted as adviser to Federal Secretary of War Edwin M. Stanton.

although the evening before I seemed to be opposed to an attack on San Antonio. He said to me, "You, young man, in that corner, what have you to say on the subject?"

I then got up and said that notwithstanding the deference which I was willing and ready to pay to the opinions of my brother Engineers, still on this occasion I was compelled to differ with them *in toto!* that ever since the night of the 7th, I had been busily engaged reconnoitering the enemy's works on the Southern part of the city, and I had seen them increasing hourly almost, in profile, development and armament, at present offering, I thought, greater obstacles to overcome than did Churubusco, the ground in front of them being entirely open to the enemy's view, almost entirely overflowed and entirely cut up with deep ditches; that, moreover, they could not by any possiblility be taken in flank or rear, which was, after all, our most successful tactic with the Mexicans. The enemy seeming to expect an attack in that direction, had made all the necessary preparations to give us a warm welcome and for that very reason, we ought to attack elsewhere, for it was one of the wisest military maxims, "never to do what your enemy expects and wishes you to do." That all military authorities fully agreed that the best way of attacking a large city, not sufficiently armed and garrisoned, is to make the strongest demonstration practicable at one of its points, and then, by a rapid movement during the night, to attack suddenly at about daybreak some other more or less remote point, at the same time keeping up a simulated attack at the original point selected. That as the General in Chief had stated by so doing, we would moreover have the advantage of making the real attack on that part of the city which offered the greatest facilities for the construction of batteries (if required) and the movement of troops; that moreover, by taking Chapultepec, we then had a strong pivot upon which to move upon any part of the

71

circumference of the city—even, if we had again to attack finally, those very same Southern gates!

My reasons, I must confess, coincided very fully with those of the General in Chief as far as he had expressed them, for I think I had gone more fully into the details of the case, but these opinions of mine had been formed long before I had ever heard him say a word on the subject, and under no consideration whatever, would I have recommended the attack on those Southern gates—and my surprise was great indeed to find that the other Engineer officers thought otherwise!

After I had spoken a dead silence ensued. General Scott then asked if any one had anything further to say. It was then that General Pierce got up and with his usual modesty and decision of character "begged that he would be permitted to change his views, after what he had just heard—for he was now in favor of the attack by Chapultepec!" The General in Chief after waiting a while longer to see if any of the Generals present would also change their minds—then got up, drew himself up to his full height and said with his imperative tone, "Gentlemen, we will attack by the Western gates! The General officers present will remain here for further orders—the meeting is dissolved." A few days afterwards meeting with General Pierce, whom I knew only by sight, he came to me and said, "Sir, I am happy to make your acquaintance, for I will always remember that opinion of yours at Piedad." And indeed he has not forgotten it, for he has often since referred to it—as I am informed.[46]

On the 24th of September,[47] after having entered the City

[46] During the remainder of the war, Beauregard and Pierce saw each other frequently, and struck up a warm friendship. When Pierce became the Democratic presidential candidate in 1852, Beauregard supported him publicly.

[47] The reader will note that Beauregard is here going ahead of his

of Mexico, I was ordered to accompany the General in Chief
to Chapultepec, where he was going to visit the fields of battle,
before finishing his report of the operations against the City
of Mexico. Whilst riding out of the City by the San Cosme road,
when near the *garita,* he called to me to come to him. I was
then in front of him with Mr. Trist and Colonel Hitchcock
—and he had on each side of him Generals Twiggs and Smith.
As I approached him, he said to me, "Young man, I wish to
reprimand you! Take your place by me, and I am only sorry
that the *whole army* is not present to listen to me; but these two
Generals will represent it! Why did you give me the advice to
attack by the Western gates? You now see the consequences!
We have taken this great city and the halls of the Montezumas,
after only a few hours of hard fighting and with only about
800 men killed and wounded." These are, I believe, his own
words as Generals Twiggs and Smith will testify to. I have
no doubt I was, as it may well be imagined, rather taken aback
at first at this unlooked for *reprimand;* but I soon replied "that
I had only had the good luck to coincide with him in opinion
on the true point of attack; for, the honor of having selected it
belonged entirely to himself and not to me and that I hoped
his views and plans would always be crowned with as complete and glorious a success."

I then left him to resume my former place, flattering myself
with the vain illusion that in his coming report he would de-
vote at least one line or a short paragraph to the humble Lieutenant of Engineers, who, alone, had supported his views with
some arguments! But I was again doomed to be disappointed;
—not one word appeared in said report, distinguishing me from
the general praise bestowed on all the Engineer officers, and

---

story in time in order to record Scott's approval of his advice at the council.

why was I forgotten? Because I had not the impudence to say to him, "General, I hope you will not forget this praise in your forthcoming report."

But to return to our subject.

On the evening of the 11th, I put Steptoe's [48] battery of two 12-pound and two 24-pound howitzers in position to fire in the morning against the works at San Antonio. In the selection of its site I was much assisted by Captain Magruder, who had his battery not far from that point the greater part of the day. And it proved to be a most excellent one, for although firing at the guns in position at the *garita*, we had not a single piece dismounted and very few men killed or wounded. The other Engineer officers went to establish and construct these batteries against Chapultepec, which opened during the day (the 12th) and the General in Chief determined to assault Chapultepec that night but some unforeseen delays occurring in the necessary arrangements, it had to be delayed until morning. I was that afternoon ordered to report to General Pillow, and Tower to General Quitman as their Engineer officers—Lee remaining with the headquarters for occurrences as they might turn up.

[48] Captain E. J. Steptoe, Third Artillery.

The Battle of Chapultepec
SEPTEMBER 12–13, 1847

ON the evening of the 12th at about 8 h. Generals Worth,
Pillow, and Quitman came to the General in Chief's
quarters with the above Engineer officers to receive their orders
for the morning attack on the Castle, their movements after
its fall being left to be determined upon after the event; it being understood, however, that the attack upon the City was to
follow immediately after the fall of the Castle. There was a
long discussion as to the best mode of proceeding, the General
in Chief listening attentively to what each one of them had to
say on the subject; concluding at last by giving each one his
orders in that clear and precise style which could seldom be
misunderstood, and which seemed to provide so well for all

75

coming events, leaving to each one, however, a certain discretionary power to act as circumstances might best direct.

Worth had at first but a secondary part to perform, forming as it were a sort of support to Pillow's attack on the Castle of Chapultepec. The latter General was to storm said Castle from the buildings of Molino del Rey, which he occupied. General Quitman, who had that day made a very gallant and close reconnoissance of the enemy's battery at the foot of Chapultepec, commanding the road thence to Tacubaya, had orders to storm that battery, for which purpose a storming party of about 250 men had been ordered to report to him from Twiggs's veteran division whilst one of the same strength had also been ordered from Worth's to report to General Pillow! Later in the evening, I believe, or early in the morning of the 13th, Smith's brigade was also ordered from the village of Piedad to the support of Quitman's division on the Tacubaya road.

The description of these two attacks are so fully given in Ripley's history of that War, that I refer anyone to it for further information should it be desired; I will here take the opportunity to state, however, that as far as I have been able to judge, that work is the only accurate military history of that war, which I have yet seen; its style being clear and concise, its description of the battles spirited and generally correct, and the author's appreciation of them and his military criticisms of the operations of those campaigns, being in most cases able and judicious; but his partiality and partisanship to the General in whose staff he was, are but too glaringly apparent, not to be decidedly condemned by an impartial judge.[49] His sneers and ungenerous allusions to the gallant and meritorious commander of the Cerro Gordo division (Twiggs), whenever he has to

[49] R. S. Ripley, the author of the work cited in note 21, was a member of Pillow's staff; his history was strongly prejudiced in that general's favor.

76

refer to him, are entirely unworthy of the author and in direct opposition to the truth of history—for I am confident that all those who had the honor of serving under that General officer would gladly testify (if it were required) not only to the superior discipline and efficiency of his division, but to his coolness and decision under trying circumstances.

But to return: At about 10 h. P. M. I commenced, with two German companies from Pennsylvania, belonging I believe to one of the new regiments, to repair the two batteries near Molino del Rey, which had fired all that day against the Castle. In my search in the dark for sand bags and other materials for that purpose, I was very much assisted by Lieutenant Ripley of Pillow's staff—for I was comparatively but little acquainted with those premises—I did not get through with these batteries until about $4\frac{1}{2}$ A. M.; for these new levies, not understanding anything about the construction of sand-bag parapets and embrasures, did not as a matter of course, progress very rapidly. I fortunately however found two or more masons amongst them, who assisted me in building up the angles and cheeks of the embrasures; but for several hours, I had to handle these sand-bags myself and the natural consequence was, that by the time we had got through, I could not very well have *run a quarter race*.

After dismissing the working party, I repaired to General Pillow's quarters at the Molinos and laid myself down on a part of Captain Hooker's [50] blanket to take a little rest before we were aroused for the hard day's work we had before us. In about an hour the servants brought in the coffee and we all took *a hasty cup of it* [51] and then commenced making the neces-

[50] Joseph Hooker, the Federal commander of the Army of the Potomac who was defeated by Lee at Chancellorsville.

[51] At the beginning of the war General Scott and President Polk (or the Secretary of War acting for the President) had exchanged several

sary preparations for the attack, which was to commence about 8 h. from a signal at general headquarters. At about that hour, the much looked-for signal was made!

On the evening before, whilst at general headquarters with General Pillow (Worth and Quitman having already left) we were invited by the General in Chief to come into supper with himself and Mr. Trist. We ate quite heartily and drank one or two toasts to our future success. On leaving at about 9 h. General Pillow inquired of General Scott if there were any necessity that I should lead the storming column? He replied, "No, Sir, I think not, the ground is perfectly clear and open to view, and the column cannot miss its way; however, employ him as you think best; but I have a request to make of you, General. *Spare my Engineer officers;* for I may have still need of them hereafter and we have already lost two." I confess that I did not feel much sorrow at having lost that honor—although as circumstances did turn out, I got into the work at its head! thus proving that *"L'homme propose et Dieu dispose."*

On arriving at the foot of the hill with General Pillow, where our skirmishers were already engaged with the enemy's forces occuping that forest of magnificent cypress-trees, he mounted his horse and turned to the left with one or two of his aides following him on foot, whilst his other aide, Passed-Midshipman

---

bitter letters concerning the general's role in the war. Scott began one epistle with the statement that he had received a message from Polk as he was sitting down to take "a hasty plate of soup." This unfortunate statement, implying that his labors did not permit him to eat properly, brought down much ridicule upon the general. By underlining his own similar expression, Beauregard was indulging in a sly dig at his superior. Considering that he intended to circulate his manuscript among army people, the allusion was very indiscreet. Scott was highly sensitive about the episode.

The Battle of Chapultepec

Rogers (of Vera Cruz memory) [52] and myself joined the party on the right, commanded by Lieutenant Colonel Johnston of the Voltigeurs.[53] After awhile falling in with two pieces of the mountain howitzers-battery under the charge of a sergeant (its commanding officer Lieutenant Reno [54] being on the left of the attack with the two other pieces, was severely wounded, as I was afterwards informed), I took charge of them and aimed one of them myself upon the enemy occupying a small lunette on the slope of the hill, until having exhausted its cartridges and our advancing forces masking their fire, I left them and repaired towards the right of the Voltigeurs, near the camp leading up to the Castle, Mr. Rogers and myself sending forward into the forest and encouraging along the road, those men who had not the intrepidity of their comrades, who were getting ahead of them.

We then reached the head of the battalion and found the gallant Colonel Johnston and his officers encouraging their no less gallant men forward, on the side of the hill, against as terrible a fire as I had yet seen! the enemy occupying their parapets a short distance in front of them, in such numbers that they could not be counted, although they could distinctly be seen from their breast up; at times, the top of the parapet was one continued sheet of flame and the whole presented as grand and sublime a scene as I have ever yet witnessed; and I will here remark, that with the exception of the Rifle Regiment, I never

[52] In the siege of Vera Cruz R. C. Rogers was in a naval group that tried to blow up a Mexican powder magazine. He was captured and later exchanged.

[53] The Voltigeur Regiment operated as two detachments, one of which was led by Joseph E. Johnston. Theoretically, the regiment was made up of an equal number of riflemen and foot soldiers; actually it was an infantry outfit.

[54] Jesse L. Reno, later a Union general.

saw new troops behave as well as this Voltigeur battalion under such trying circumstances and they did infinite credit to their officers.

Rogers and myself having no special duty to attend to or orders to communicate, everything going on as well and briskly as the circumstances of the case permitted, took a half dozen of the Voltigeurs immediately around us, and by exciting them a little (and ourselves too) by a few cheers and word of encouragement, got them to *within 100 yards* of the parapets of the work—but when we had got there, the fire was so intense and appalling (representing to my mind a tempest at sea with the wind howling, hissing and whizzing through the cordage) that we at first had a little difficulty in getting our men to continue their rapid and destructive fire. Feeling the importance of their doing so, and the sooner the better, Rogers and myself took their rifles in succession and made them load for us from behind a low rock; which however was only an imaginary protection (for it was not over two feet high) and they were either standing or kneeling behind it. But in a very few minutes their confidence was restored and they fired as coolly and deliberately as though they were aiming at targets! which proves, that under such exciting circumstances, very few men, if properly managed, are not susceptible of the greatest display of physical courage.

About this time, hearing Colonel Johnston (than whom there are, *if any,* few better or braver officers) and some of his subalterns telling their men to fire quickly and take good aim —I turned round and cried out to him as loud as I could, until I had drawn his attention (for the firing of the infantry and artillery, the hissing of the balls, etc. was perfectly deafening) and knowing the effect which such a demonstration under those circumstances would create in our favor, I said to him, holding at the time a loaded rifle in my hand, which I was about to fire, "Colonel, what will you bet on this shot?" He quickly replied, "A picayune, payable in the City of Mexico." (or, he may have said: "Drinks in the City of Mexico," I cannot now recollect which), I then took deliberate aim, fired and cried out to him, "You have lost, you will have to pay it!"

Now this was not done through a spirit of boasting as would at first sight appear, but merely to encourage the men around us and inspire them with a little more confidence, by showing them that there was no more danger while shooting than while being quietly shot at! and I flatter myself with the hope that it had the desired effect; for not long after, we had so far silenced the enemy's artillery and infantry fire, that the order to charge was given to the storming column, which was a little to our left, waiting for its ladders and the favorable moment to make the rush on the salient of the work pointing towards them.

Rogers and myself having heard the order to *charge*, left the Voltigeurs and ran across the space which separated us from it. In doing so we passed over a certain number of *mounds of earth and stone,* which I mistook at the time for *graves,* but afterwards to my *horror,* found they were the *mines* or *fougasses,* which they had prepared to blow us up with—but fortunately did not or could not explode them in time! We reached the head of the column as it was placing its ladders in the ditch and across it and as soon as I could find the chance, rushed across one of the latter. I remember distinctly that it vacillated considerably and came very near throwing me into the ditch which was also filled with our men trying to get up the other ladders, and their bayonets under me looked like anything but a *bed of feathers!* Rogers in attemping to follow me fell into the ditch, but fortunately for him, along the side of the counterscarp, which was partially clear of bayonets.

I then jumped over the parapet wall (not over four of five feet high) and found inside of it one or two officers and a few men (about a dozen) who had just preceded me—who those officers were I did not take time to consider; but think from what I heard afterwards that one was Lieutenant Armistead of the infantry and the other Captain Biddle of the Voltigeurs.[55] I immediately passed on however, making a rush for the first open door of the citadel, followed by two or three soldiers— my intention being at the time to take down that Mexican flag, which was waving so gracefully and gently upon all that scene of carnage and bloodshed which was going on under its very shadow! I suddenly found myself in a perfectly dark room with all its doors strongly barricaded! As I rushed in, some Mexicans who were in it, rushed out, but only to fall into the hands of those who were following me.

Finding no stairs or opening in that room, I came out of it to go into some other entrance; but as I came out, I saw one of our soldiers, who seemed to be perfectly exasperated, about to run his bayonet through the neck of a young Mexican officer, who stood in front of him without hat or sword! I mechanically struck a heavy blow with my sabre upon the bayonet, which was about to perform its bloody and deadly deed, and had the good luck to parry the thrust so far as only to let it run through his military coat collar and cravat. I then rebuked the soldier, placed the officer in charge of a sentinel and ascertained that his name was Mr. Ximenes, a young Lieutenant of the Corps of Engineers.

By this time the work was filled with our own troops, whilst the enemy, who had taken refuge in the citadel, continued to fire upon us from the windows of the second story and the roof—but we made another charge into some other parts of the building and after bursting open the doors of several

[55] Lewis A. Armistead, Sixth Infantry; Charles J. Biddle. Armistead is the Confederate officer who was killed while leading the vanguard of "Pickett's charge" at Gettysburg.

rooms filled with Mexican soldiers on their knees praying for mercy, and placing sentinels to protect them (whilst they little deserved it, after the cruel treatment of our wounded at Molino del Rey) I left them to search again for those stairs I had been looking for. I at last found them and rushed up them faster than I had ever ascended any flight of stairs before—but arrived only in time to see that Mexican tricolored flag being hauled down by Captain Barnard [56] of the Voltigeurs and a few others. Those Mexican prisoners had been the cause of my disappointment, thus proving again, that *"L'homme propose et Dieu dispose."*

All that I have just related may appear at first sight as rather highly wrought; but it is nothing more than the plain unvarnished facts as they occurred and as the persons to whom I have referred can testify to at any time. It might perhaps have been more to my praise not to have stated them so plainly; but besides that the truth in this instance can do no harm. Those who are sufficiently well acquainted with me, know that I am not apt to boast of them; but if it appears singular, it must be ascribed entirely to the circumstances under which it happened —for I must not be understood to *intimate even* that others did not do as much, if not more than myself; far from me any such idea, for I am fully aware that, to accomplish what we did in that war, each one of us had to use his best exertions—and I have only given mine here. I had taken the firm resolution on going into that campaign, that no one of my grade in the service should surpass me in zeal and activity. Whether I have succeeded, I will leave others to determine.

[56] John G. Barnard, who in the Civil War was McClellan's chief of engineers in the Army of the Potomac.

The Belen Garita
SEPTEMBER 13, 1847

A SHORT time after the pulling down of the Mexican flag, perhaps about five minutes (it is very difficult, when events succeed each other so rapidly, to keep the run of time) we saw the enemy retreating from about the battery attacked by General Quitman's forces, and as they passed within range of us, we opened upon them from the top of the hill, to increase their speed a little. Afterwards, seeing a column of our troops moving in pursuit of them along the Belen road, Rogers (who had again joined me) and I, thinking they might possibly belong to a part of Pillow's column, which might have followed the road at the foot of the Chapultepec hill, con-

84

cluded that we had better join it, as we had not seen the General since we had parted from him at the beginning of the battle! To shorten the distance, however, we jumped out of one of the eastern windows of the citadel, facing over a very precipitous side of the hill; we succeeded in getting to the bottom by letting ourselves down from rock to rock, not however without running the risk of being shot at as Mexican officers trying to make their escape.

We reached the head of the column and found to our surprise that it belonged to General Quitman's command. On meeting with the General himself, I ascertained from him that his Engineer officer, Lieutenant Tower, had been put *"hors de combat"* by a wound in the head, received during the gallant attack of the lower battery. I offered then to remain with him, provided he would give me the order, for otherwise I would have to return to General Pillow's command. He immediately did so. Lieutenant Rogers then left me, and I told him to present my compliments to General Pillow, whom I did not know to be wounded at the time, and to inform him, that, as I supposed I had got through with him, I had reported to General Quitman in Lieutenant Tower's place, and probably would not see him again until we had reached "the halls of the Montezumas."

It has been a question of much controversy to determine which was carried first—the Castle attacked by General Pillow or the battery at its foot commanding the Tacubaya road and attacked by General Quitman. When such important dramas are being enacted, it is not at all surprising that the actors in them should differ as to what takes place on other parts of the scene on which they are immediately performing—for unless they are mere idlers or lookers-on, their attention is too much taken up with what takes place immediately around them to allow them much time or leisure in observing minutely what is occurring elsewhere. It is unquestionable, however, that the fall of the above positions taking place in such rapid succession did not have much influence in the operations against each other, although their *simultaneous attack* no doubt had a considerable one.

In a strategic point of view, as a matter of course, the fall of the Castle had to bring with it the evacuation of the lower battery which was commanded by the former—but that it had that effect at the time is doubtful, for the reason that when the Mexican forces retreated from the lower battery and the aqueduct (along which they were formed in line of battle) a part of them retreated inside of the wall at the foot of the Chapultepec hill and they were driven from thence by our firing from the Castle; thus showing that they were not conscious of the fall of the latter. This I saw myself and can vouch for. Whether the one or the other fell first, I consider immaterial; for the *success* at either point had no influence whatever on the result of the attack at the other, as the enemy had not the time to be influenced by becoming aware of it.

With this column I had the pleasure of meeting with Generals Smith and Shields, the latter although severely wounded in the forearm, still keeping the command of his brigade. Whilst the column was being organized for the attack of the middle battery enfilading the road—General Quitman and myself went on top of what was known as the "Conference house" (of armistice recollections) [57] and had a full view of the positions in front of us although exposed to a severe fire of grape from them. We then came down and going on the other side of the aqueduct (on stone-arches in the middle of the road along which our column was forming and moving slowly)—I saw lying

[57] The reference is to a building in which American and Mexican representatives had met to arrange an armistice after the battle of Churubusco.

across the canal along side of the road, a tree (or I had it cut down, I do not now recollect) on which I crossed to examine the ground on the left of that battery. Taking advantage of the tall prairie grass which grew alongside of the bank of said canal, I ascertained that the battery could be taken in flank and turned in that direction. In attempting to recross in a hurry, I slipt from the tree and fell into the canal! Fortunately, however, I caught one of the branches and got out.

I then endeavored to get a company of the column to accompany me again across the canal to make that flank attack; but the officer commanding that portion of the column refused his consent unless the authority of General Quitman could be obtained for such a movement! this too whilst the attack in front was about to commence and I had hardly time to obtain that order! Do you think that officer had the soul of his profession in him? No—he was "food for powder" and nothing else.

What his name is, I do not think it is worth the while to endeavor to remember. I then left him—to get the order, but when I arrived at the head of the column, we were so near the battery and the impetus so great that I kept on with it and we took it without much resistance. It was here that for the first time I made my acquaintance with a Mexican ball! One grazed my shoulder leaving its mark on it and the other wounded me slightly in the thigh.

After taking that battery, as the firing from three pieces in position at the *garita* about 700 yards in front of us was very intense, and they could not be turned on account of the low and marshy ground, covered with water, on each side of our road or causeway here—I thought of taking advantage of the open aqueduct which passed along the middle of said causeway, by making a hole in it to let out its water and advancing a column *in it* to open down upon the gunners in that

87

battery, a close and well aimed fire. But upon examining it with the assistance of Lieutenant Coppie [58] of the Artillery and some soldiers, I found that this trough was too narrow for that purpose, whilst it was exposed to be enfiladed by the shells from the citadel about three or four hundred yards in rear of the *garita* battery, and it was also commanded at the latter point by the Mexican infantry on the top or *azotea* of the *garita* house, so I gave up this idea.

A short time after, whilst waiting in rear of the battery we had taken, for the column to close up before making the attack on the battery in front of us, Generals Quitman, Shields, Smith, several aides and myself were conversing on various subjects; a howitzer-shell fired from the Citadel came and struck the upper edge of the aqueduct immediately above our heads (not over six or seven feet) exploding at the same time—covering us with "debris" of masonry. The concussion was so great that it threw some and severely stunned others, but fortunately killed or wounded none. If it had passed five or six inches farther to our side it would have fallen into the very midst of us—and it would have been about the most effective shot they had yet sent us.

Not long after this General Smith observing the movement of some troops about the Paseo which seemed to be directed towards our left and rear, and seeing that I had my spy-glass, called my attention to them, saying at the same time, "Let us go forward a little and observe what they are about." This was at about 12½ h. P. M., and I am under the impression that it was the force which Santa Anna had kept all the morning at the *garita* of San Antonio in front of one of Twiggs's brigades, believing the true attack to take place at that point, whilst the one against Chapultepec was only a feint. But at that

[58] This officer, whom Beauregard refers to here and later as Coppie, was undoubtedly Henry Coppée.

88

time being undeceived and finding that we had taken the latter place and were moving on rapidly to the attack of the *garitas* of Belen and San Cosme (the latter by Worth) he was then very likely bringing up his forces to put them in position at these two points. Having ordered General Teres [59] to hold out to the last at the first of the *garitas,* assisted by the citadel immediately in its rear—he was then going in person to oppose Worth at the other, and this no doubt was the movement which had attracted Smith's attention. Quitman at the time was, I believe, making his preparations for the attack on the *garita* battery.

Smith and myself passed in front of our captured battery and stepped into or about the middle of the road which every now and then was swept with grape from the two pieces which enfiladed it. As I was looking through my spy-glass at Santa Anna and his troops, we were no doubt seen at the *garita* battery, for they opened upon us and the grape came rushing and whizzing around us at a furious rate. As the thought flashed across my mind that we were spared this time again! a smaller grape which was lagging behind, came and struck the hilt of my sabre, then my side and stunned me severely for a while —taking all the breath out of my body—but I soon recovered my strength (partly due no doubt to a drink of good brandy or whiskey given to me by one of the General's aides) and I examined my side supposing I had a hole in it at least large enough to receive my fist—so severe had been the concussion! but it had only penetrated my coat pocket where my thick gloves and eye glasses had no doubt stopped its onward course! at which I felt considerably relieved; and I sat down in one of the arches of the aqueduct revolving in my mind whether I would be able to endure a few more shocks of that kind, and if at any rate I could go any further. Glory at that time, I must confess, had lost many of its charms! Besides, it must be remembered

[59] A. Terrés.

that I had been up all that night preceding, piling up sand bags on top of each other.

In the meantime the column was again set in motion to attack the *garita* battery and as I saw my friends passing by where I sat, my spirits began to revive and I commenced feeling a certain desire *to see* what was going to take place. About this time Captain Drum and Benjamin [60] passed with their pieces (one 24-pound howitzer and one long 18-pound) one on each side of the aqueduct, firing as they advanced, notwithstanding the shower of grape and canister, solid shot and shells, which was pouring upon them. This was rather too glorious for me to lose the sight of, so I got up very sore all over it is true, but still much stronger than I had expected—and I followed them, keeping, however, under cover of the side piers of the aqueduct.

After advancing some distance, Drum not seeing the arrival of the ammunition which he had ordered, asked me to relieve him a moment, whilst he went to see why it was not forthcoming. Of course such a request from such a gallant fellow could not be refused, so I took his place and did my best to repay the Mexicans for the condition I was in at the time (as Lieutenant Coppie and others can testify to if needed). Drum however soon returned and retook his place, whilst I continued as before along the aqueduct, until the excitement increasing upon me, cured me of my temporary pains, and I repaired again towards the head of the column to take a part in the attack. But when I got there they had just taken possession of it, General Quitman and Lieutenant Stevens [61] of the Rifles, being the first to mount on the parapets of the battery—the General then using his handkerchief as our colors to proclaim that we

[60] Lieutenant Calvin Benjamin.
[61] This officer has not been identified.

90

had at last set our feet in the City of Mexico! It was then 1:20 h. P. M.

Drum then took possession of the eight pounder which had been captured, turned it around on its own platform against a battery near the citadel and after having lost twice nearly all the men at his piece, fell himself mortally wounded by a shot which broke both of his legs! and thus perished one of the most gallant and promising young officers of the army! A few moments afterwards, his Lieutenant (Mr. Benjamin) having advanced with his own piece beyond the *garita* battery, after also having nearly all his men killed and wounded, was also mortally wounded! This was another severe loss to the service.

During the advance along the Causeway, one of Benjamin's men, becoming terrified at the awful discharges of grape, canister, etc. which were being poured upon them from the two pieces in position in front of them, took refuge in one of the arches of the aqueduct and when called back to his piece did not move with much alacrity, as may well be supposed. The sergeant at the piece, who was already wounded in the leg, but had bound it up hastily with his handkerchief went up to him and repeated the order—but the other not obeying with sufficient zeal, the *Sergeant* drew his sabre and under a shower of grape, laid it severely once or twice on his shoulders and brought him back to his piece! With such noncommissioned officers what would not an army do? This I *saw* myself, there is no hearsay about it.

From the beginning of my acquaintance with Captain Drum at Cerro Gordo, I had always looked upon him as one of the most promising officers of his grade; his gallantry was only equaled by his modesty—and I would consider him a very great loss to the country, if true merit and worth were a criterion to rank and command in the service.

91

Not long after taking the *garita,* I received orders from General Quitman to put up a battery for two guns between the *garita* house and the aqueduct. I told him that without the sappers I did not think it could be done; for there were at least five or six guns in battery at the citadel playing upon us with grape and canister at about 350 yards; but as he seemed anxious to have it done, so as to open a fire against them as soon as practicable, I told him, however, that if he desired it I would try it, provided he would send me a working party of about forty men. This was immediately done; but unfortunately (or more like *fortunately*) this detail was again of the new levies or volunteers. The attempt, as a matter of course, proved unsuccessful and the construction of the battery was delayed until night.

We all then took cover, as well as we could, behind the *garita* house, and the parapet of its battery, as well as behind a small sand-bag parapet for the infantry, which General Quitman had thrown up very judiciously on the right of the aqueduct towards the Piedad road, immediately after we had taken possession of this position and at the time I was endeavoring to construct that battery already spoken of. Whilst lying down by the side of General Smith and staff and several officers of his command, under cover of the *garita* house—I saw him perform one of the coolest and most gallant acts of the whole war. I mean, as a matter of course, of those which came under my observation.

Between the battery at this point, and the aqueduct (on our left of the latter) there was an opening of about twelve feet, through which carriages, carts, etc. were allowed to pass, when going to or coming from Chapultepec. This opening was completely swept by some of the guns of the citadel with grape and canister and by the fire of their sharp shooters, from behind the arches of the aqueduct under the protection of the former; so that it was a matter of life and death to pass this Thermopilea [sic], in going from one side of our position to the other, and in which the latter (death) had all the advantages.

One of the General's riflemen, in endeavoring to pass this opening, started diagonally across it and leisurely, instead of taking the shortest line and at double quick time! He was told to run to get out of the dangerous pass as quickly as possible; but he seemed perfectly indifferent to the shower of projectiles of all sorts which was passing about him at the time. He had not proceeded far however, on his dangerous walk, when he received a shot in the side and fell immediately. He raised himself on his elbow once or twice as though endeavoring to get up, but without uttering a word or a groan! General Smith immediately ordered a party "to go and bring in that wounded man." Several soldiers jumped up and stepped eagerly to his rescue, but they had no sooner got to that fatal opening, than they came to a sudden stop—the fate of each one seemed to stare him in the face. General Smith immediately repeated the order in a little firmer voice, which made them advance a step or two, but they again halted to await a more favorable opportunity to get to their comrade.

The General then got up, unbuckled his sabre and without uttering another word or giving another order, quickly marched to his wounded rifleman—caught hold of him by his shoulder and commenced dragging him under cover! In an instant officers and men rushed to his aid, and never before, I dare say, was a wounded soldier carried off a field of battle by such gallant hands! but strange to say, notwithstanding the critical position in which they were all, not one of them was hurt—the enemy having about that time left a short interval between his discharges of artillery and musketry—as he occasionally did, to allow the smoke to be blown away. They had only brought in a corpse however! for he was laid by the side of me (I was then

suffering considerably from pain and fatigue, all excitement
having disappeared) and he died a few moments afterwards!
Such is the secret of General Smith's popularity with his officers and men.

The enemy kept up their fire upon us until dark, making
in the meantime one or two attempts to dislodge us, finding
that we had almost entirely ceased firing on our side (from the
want of ammunition); but they were sent back faster than
they had come. I saw during that afternoon one of their solid
shots ricochet in one of the arches of the aqueduct where our
men had placed themselves under cover—and it killed and
wounded five or six of them.

A little after dark I informed General Quitman that I was
ready to commence the construction of that battery. He told
me then that he was anxious to have another one placed for one
gun on the right of the aqueduct; but I told him that the
materials we had there would hardly answer for the first one.
He then ordered me to take for the other one, the sand bags
of the infantry parapet which he had had thrown up that afternoon—to which however I objected as it was too much needed
for the protection of our infantry—for, I remarked, "Artillery
cannot protect itself." He then after a while, gave it up, notwithstanding its importance and his desire to have it constructed.
But about that time one of his aides (Lieutenant Lovell or
Wilcox) [62] having informed us that he had noticed a large
quantity of sand-bags at the battery taken at the foot of Chapultepec—he was sent for them.

At the same time, I sent word to Captain Lee to send an
officer of Engineers to relieve me, as I could not bear up much
longer against the pain and fatigue from which I was then
suffering, but he not long after sent me word that he had no
one to send, as Lieutenant Stevens had been wounded when

[62] Mansfield Lovell; Cadmus Wilcox.

with Worth's column near the San Cosme Causeway—himself had been badly hurt—and Lieutenants Smith and McClellan were with their sapper-company, as busy as they could be, near the *garita* of San Cosme, and that I must endeavor to hold out till morning! I must confess I felt rather desperate at the prospect before me—but as there was no help for it—it became useless to say anything more on the subject. So after taking a cup of coffee, which General Quitman had the kindness to offer me (and which was the only thing I had taken since the one that morning at General Pillow's quarters) we went together in front of our battery to look for the site of that second one he desired to have constructed.

As we were feeling our way or groping along in the dark—the General contending that there was a little high ground in our front which we might take advantage of, and I pertinaciously denying it, I suddenly saw him disappear almost headforemost in front of me and I felt myself falling into some unknown cavity. I made a terrible effort to recover myself and came down feet foremost into the water up to my waist. We then found ourselves to be in the canal along the Piedad Causeway at its junction with the one at the *garita,* and I then asked the General what he thought of his *high ground!* He at once admitted laughingly that it was a d——d sight lower than I had said. We got out, however, dripping wet and chose a position for the battery not far from the scene of *our ducking.*

About one hour afterwards, I was at work with about 90 or 100 men divided off into two relieves for each battery, and by daylight they were completed, with their guns in position, and matches lighted! the one on the left of the aqueduct being made for one 24-pound howitzer (Drum's) and the other for one 18-pound (Benjamin's), all three pieces being embrasures. Now, how did I accomplish that much in one night? By remembering that in our column I had seen Lieutenants H. Coppie, First

Artillery and W. H. Wood, Third Infantry (than whom there are few better or more efficient officers) who had been my assistants three months at Tampico, whilst constructing its defenses a few months before. I sent for them and asked them if they were willing to assist me. Their answer, as a matter of course, was in the affirmative—and nobly did they redeem their promise, for as I stated before, the two batteries were ready before daylight and too much praise cannot be bestowed on these two young officers, especially the latter.

I had been two days and two nights on my feet, without sitting down more than a few hours in that whole time, and in the last thirty-six hours I had only taken two cups of coffee! I had also fallen twice into the canals without even having a blanket or overcoat to cover myself with afterwards!

As soon as the batteries were completed (a little before daybreak) I turned them over to my friend Captain Steptoe of the artillery, who was to command them, that he might put in the platforms; for I could then hold out no longer and wanted to take a little rest before the day work should commence again. So I took a seat under the gallery of the *garita* and endeavored to sleep awhile; but I was so exhausted and so cold (being still wet through and through up to my waist), that I was unable to do so—and to go into the warmer atmosphere of the *garita* house, where were huddled together a large number of officers and men, who had taken up their quarters there during the night, which was extremely cold for that period of the year, but there I could hardly find a place even to stand upon!

The Capture of Mexico City
SEPTEMBER 14, 1847

AT about daylight on the 14th when on the point of open-ing the fire of our batteries upon the citadel, a white flag appeared in that direction, coming to announce that the Mexi-can army had abandoned it as well as the city during the night, leaving an officer in charge of the citadel to surrender it to us. As I was the only staff officer present who could speak the Spanish language, I was sent with Lieutenant Lovell, one of General Quitman's aides, to see if the information was correct; the bearer of the flag being kept as a hostage until our return. Upon entering the citadel, the officer left in charge of it, offering to turn over everything, *provided we would furnish him with our receipts!* I looked at him in utter amazement and finally told him that in such cases, we "gave our receipts with the points of our swords! That if he did not give up the property under his charge willingly, we would *take it.*" He then made a bow and gave that eternal answer, *"Para servir a Vmds., Señores."* [63] Lovell then made the signal we had agreed upon, and our troops marched in, taking possession of the citadel, the property, the documents and the officer!

During the storming of the *garita* battery, one of General Quitman's aides, Lieutenant Wilcox, received a musket ball on the side of his Colt's revolver which was hanging to his waist belt. The shock was so strong that it knocked him down and bruised him severely—but he soon recovered from it. The ball which was picked up by the side of him presented a remarkable appearance. It had been flattened to about the thickness of a dollar and had printed on its side the name of the maker of the pistol and the place where it was made! General Quitman's aide, Lieutenant Van Dorn,[64] was wounded in the foot—and I believe very few of us got off without some bruise or other. It was emphatically a hot place; so much so, that some of the most timid expressed the opinion that General Quitman ought to abandon it; but he never for an instant entertained that idea.

A short while before sunset [on September 13] a wagon of ammunition came trotting down the road on the south side of the aqueduct, and notwithstanding the signs which were made to him [the driver] to halt some distance from the *garita,* he continued on, until he came up to where we were under shelter of the battery. He was then told to turn immediately around and go back, for the enemy would soon open upon him, but the road being too narrow at that point he could not do so.

[63] "At your service, Sirs."

[64] In the Civil War Earl Van Dorn was a Confederate general, and in 1862 served under Beauregard in the West.

He was then ordered to unhitch his mules and go off with them—but before he could do so his wagon having been observed from a battery near the citadel, one or two guns were opened upon him with grape. In a few rounds two of his mules were killed—and when we told him to take shelter in one of the arches a few feet from him, he said, "No, I want to get my mules," and he went on unhitching them until he had succeeded in freeing the other two, he then started with them down the road towards Chapultepec, as fast as they could go, and how they did not all get killed is a mystery to me.

General Worth in his report says, that on his way to San Cosme having sent Colonel Duncan with two field pieces to within 400 yards on the flank of that middle battery, attacked by Quitman, he had assisted the latter materially in taking it. Now, there is quite an error in this—and my opinion is, that this diversion of Worth's had not the slightest effect! For this reason, that the distance stated, instead of being *400* yards was *880* yards as measured by myself, when I made the "map of the city of Mexico and its defenses" now at the office of the Chief Engineer in Washington—and the position instead of being on the flank of said battery (which by the by had its flank protected by a parapet forming a traverse in that direction) was on a line forming nearly an angle of 30° [degrees] with that flanking direction—and there were at least two heavier pieces in that battery firing through embrasures. Now I think that these two last had a better chance to drive away the two under Colonel Duncan (if they could do much at that range) and the latter's guns could not possibly be got nearer, on account of the canals which intersected his line of approach in every direction.

General Scott in his report says, that during the advance on the Belen Causeway he had sent instructions to General Quitman not to push on too boldly, as his attack was only a secondary one, Worth's being the principal one by the San Cosme Causeway, and further on he again says, that during the night of the 13th–14th, he had sent to inform him (Quitman) that Santa Anna having left the city, it had offered to surrender. Now, the above must be true, since General Scott says so, but I can assure him that no such instructions as the first one were ever received by General Quitman until after the *garita* battery had been taken, and the second one never reached him, for I was almost constantly with him and conversed with him very freely on what we had or would have to do, and he never intimated to me once, his having received any such message. Moreover, he would certainly not have kept up all night a large portion of his command, which required so much rest, constructing two batteries that were to be of no use in the morning.

After leaving a garrison at the *garita* and at the citadel, we marched towards the main plaza of the city with only about three or four regiments and Steptoe's battery! We arrived and formed in line of battle in front of the Cathedral as its clock was striking 7 A. M. The American flag was then hoisted on the Palace of the Montezumas! but through some mistake, the flag of the Rifle Regiment was first hoisted in its place by Captain Roberts! [65] General Quitman and myself then went into the Palace to see what disposition could be made of it in case of a sudden attack upon our small forces—and we three, I believe, were the first American officers who entered it.

I remember that the sight we presented marching into that immense city, being nearly all of us covered with mud, and some with blood—some limping—some with arms in scarfs —and others with heads in bandages! followed by two endless lines of gaping *leperos* and rabble was anything but glorious in

[65] Benjamin S. Roberts, Mounted Rifles.

100

appearance, for it looked more like the ridiculous than the sublime—whatever history may say to the contrary notwithstanding.

The novelty of our position had renewed my failing energies and General Quitman not having one of his personal staff about him at the time (as they were transmitting his orders in every direction) requested me to go and inform the General in Chief of our entrance into the city and of our having taken possession of the palace. It was some time before I could procure a horse for that purpose—but the General's orderly having arrived at that time, I took his horse, and shortly after having seen a Mexican horseman passing by I stopped him and gave his horse to the orderly telling the latter to accompany me.

We then rode along slowly towards the San Cosme *garita* in the deserted streets of that large Capital, as silent as the tomb—every house being strongly barricaded—with nothing to disturb this death-like stillness, but the clattering of our horses' hoofs on the pavements. I could not help remembering then the description by Prescott of Cortes' flight from this city during that celebrated *"Noche Triste"* about 317 years before—by the very road I was then travelling upon. It seemed to me that every moment I would hear the demoniacal yell of his savage and infuriated foes, when they suddenly discovered his retreat and commenced their deadly attack upon him.[66]

[66] On July 1, 1520, Hernando Cortés and his Spanish army attempted to retire from Mexico City at night. The Aztecs discovered the movement and attacked. After hard fighting the Spaniards escaped with heavy losses. In Spanish annals the disaster was known as the *noche triste*—"the sad or melancholy night." Beauregard was thinking of the description of the retreat in William H. Prescott's *History of the Conquest of Mexico*, which had been published in 1843. For Prescott's account, see the Modern Library edition of his *History of the Conquest of Mexico and History of the Conquest of Peru*, 441–53.

Beauregard in Mexico

At the corner of a street I suddenly came upon a Mexican Lancer in full costume—examining what was going on at the two extremities of the street I was following. I hesitated a moment whether I would not make a rush upon him—but after a moment's reflection, seeing that he was better mounted and armed than I was (for I lost my revolver the day before during the attack on that middle battery, where I came very near losing my sabre also) and feeling that I could hardly give a blow with my sabre, I soon gave up the idea. Moreover I was on a special errand and it was my duty to avoid any such rencontre. So I passed by him without appearing to take any notice of him and he allowed me to go by unmolested!

At the Almeda or public garden, I came upon the head of Worth's command stationed there at the time; they appeared as astonished to see me coming from that direction as I was to find them there—for I was not aware of their true position until then. When I told them of our having occupied the Palace, they appeared considerably vexed at our temerity and success. I then continued on and met General Scott and staff near the angle of the San Cosme and Chapultepec roads; it must have been about 8½ h. He appeared delighted to see me and after I had communicated to him my message, his first question was, "Whether we had been in any hurry to forestall General Worth in the occupation of the Palace."

I told him that we had never been fully aware of the position of General Worth and that I had only just ascertained it— moreover—that we had never heard of the surrender of the city until we had entered the citadel, where we met with an English gentleman (Mr. Wilson) who had to come to give us the information and to tell us to be on our guard, as it was reported that as soon as our troops would become disorganized by the exesses and depredations inherent to the taking violent possession of such a large city—a rising of the *leperos* [67] would take place during which Santa Anna, who had only retired to the small village of Guadalupe, three miles to the north of Mexico City, would suddenly return, attack us when thus unprepared to receive him, and it was hoped, that every one of us would be exterminated. This was all a very beautiful scheme, but it was frustrated by our doing the very reverse of what they expected us to do.

I then returned with the General in Chief and staff to the Palace where we arrived at about 9 h. when a salute was fired by Steptoe's battery and all the necessary orders were given for the proper occupation of the city. General Quitman (than whom there was not a more gallant officer in the service) being appointed its Governor; but before they could all be carried into execution, the outbreak spoken of took place; and by 12 h. had become so intense, that Santa Anna thought the favorable moment had arrived for carrying his scheme into execution. Unfurtunately for him the head of his column came directly upon Duncan's battery, which opened upon it a destructive fire and drove it back faster than it had come. This revolt continued until the next day about noon—and it one time looked very unfavorable. I again had the pleasure of seeing here as a mere spectacle however the gallant Cerro Gordo division (with which I had so often served that I almost considered myself as belonging to it) led on by its worthy General (Twiggs or "Old Orizaba" [68] as he was called) and doing its new kind of work —fighting in the streets—storming houses, etc. as it did everything else *"Sans peur et sans reproche."*

[67] The rabble or lowest element of the city's population.
[68] Twiggs had a way of belching forth profanity and oratory at his troops; this may have led them to call him "Old Orizaba" after the volcanic Mount Orizaba, highest peak in Mexico.

Beauregard in Mexico

A short while after reaching the Palace, I was taken down with a violent attack of fever and ague—which kept me in bed for several days and from the effects of which I did not entirely recover for several weeks.

I have now given you a perfectly faithful account of my "personal reminiscences" during the campaign; from it and my other notes, I may one of these days write down my "General Reminiscences" which I hope will be somewhat more entertaining—together with a few military criticisms on the manner of conducting its operations—for although I am a great admirer of our glorious Old Chief [69]—whom I consider the best General of the present day—still he has not been faultless and he must, as a matter or course, expect to find "a few thorns amongst the laurels" which he has so deservedly gathered. And I think if his indefatigable opponent, Santa Anna, had been a little better seconded by his lieutenants and had had better prepared materials to fight with—he would have forced him to have observed a little more closely the true principles of the art of war, on one or two occasions that he departed from them and which does not often happen with impunity in a well conducted war.

With the exception of the Mexican Engineer officers, and a few of the artillery—all the rest were of but poor account, being generally the first to abandon their posts at the very time they ought to have clung to them the closer. As to the Mexican soldier, with better discipline he would make a very efficient one—for he is materially sober and frugal—bearing fatigue and privations of all sorts with fortitude; and standing the fire of the infantry and artillery fully as well as our own troops—but from the want of discipline and proper training, he cannot stand a charge of the bayonet—which is also, no doubt, mostly due to

[69] Scott.

104

his total want of confidence in his officers and in each other—
and we know that the greatest Captain of ancient or modern
times has said, *"Que la confiance est plus de la moitie de la
Victoire."* [70]

[70] Beauregard was quoting his great hero, Napoleon: "Confidence is
more than half of Victory."

Beauregard after the War
NOVEMBER 1856–JANUARY 1857

IN 1856 Beauregard considered leaving the army. Like many other officers, he was disgusted with the low pay and the slow rate of promotion. He decided to better his fortunes by taking service with the filibuster William Walker in Nicaragua.[1] To support his application to Walker for a position, he asked various generals who had known him in Mexico to

[1] Walker was a dynamic adventurer who, in 1855, had established himself as dictator of Nicaragua. He seems to have nourished ambitions to become the head of a federation of Central American states. His extraordinary career can be traced in W. O. Scroggs, *Filibusters and Financiers* (New York, 1916).

write letters of recommendation. Quitman, Twiggs, Patterson, and P. F. Smith, readily obliged him, although Smith, who had formed a high opinion of Beauregard during the war, was distressed at the prospect of the army losing such a promising officer. So also was general in chief Scott. Both wrote Beauregard urging him to stay with the service. In the end, Beauregard, probably moved by the arguments of Scott and Smith and the hope of promotion held out by their good opinions of him, concluded not to go to Nicaragua.

He thought these letters were important enough to include copies of them at the end of his copy of the "Reminiscences." They are reproduced here because he considered they dealt with a vital phase of his career and because they throw light on the problems of a young officer in the years just preceding the Civil War.

JOHN A. QUITMAN TO WILLIAM WALKER

New Orleans Nov 22, 1856.

General,

I beg leave to present to you Major Beauregard of the Corps of Engineers, U. S. Army. Major Beauregard served under my immediate command, as principal engineer officer, in the attack upon the city of Mexico on the 13th & 14th Sept 1847—and it is but justice to him to say that his services on that trying occasion were of very great importance to our success—

He will no doubt furnish you with abundant official evidence of his valuable services in the Mexican war, and of the high estimation in which he was held by the whole army, both as an officer & man. I need only add that since that time, he has continued to retain the public confidence in his ability & integrity, having been entrusted by the Government, with important & responsible duties, both military & civil—I trust that if I can at any time be serviceable to your country, you will not hesitate to believe that my inclinations to serve you & your cause are unchanged.

With the highest respect &c
J. A. Quitman.

DAVID E. TWIGGS TO WILLIAM WALKER

New Orleans
28 Novr. 1856.

Sir

Major Beauregard of the U. S. engineer corps contemplates a visit to your country. Major B. served in the Mexican war with me, & sometimes with the Division under my command, it affords me great pleasure to say his Bravery as an officer was equal to any one in the army, & his services were *always* highly, approved & appreciated by our distinguished commander Lt Gnl Scott

With high respect
yr obt st
D. E. Twiggs
brigr Gel US Army.

WINFIELD SCOTT TO BEAUREGARD

New York, December 9, 1856.

Major P. G. T. Beauregard,
   U. States' Engineers.
   My dear Sir:
   I am much concerned to learn that you think of leaving the army after acquiring, at an early age, so much distinction in it; both for science & high gallantry in the field. Your brilliant services, in Mexico, nobody, who witnessed them, can ever forget. They bind the affections of the army to you, & ought, perhaps, to bind you to us. If you go, abroad, you will give up that connection & also a high social position at some hazard. My best

Appendix

wishes, however, will ever accompany my gallant young friend wherever he may go.

Winfield Scott.

ROBERT PATTERSON TO WILLIAM WALKER

Phila 10th. Decr 1856

Sir.

Without the honor of a personal aquaintance with you, I venture to recommend to your favor and special consideration my friend Major G. T. Beauregard of the U. S. Army who I learn has some intention of visiting Nicaragua.

It was my good fortune to have Major Beauregard under my command for sometime—at Tampico—Vera Cruz & Cerro Gordo— In point of Science Skill, Courage and all other essentials of a good officer he is the Peer of any man in the Army of the United States. If you can secure his services—you will have at the head of your Engineer Corps, a man I would pick out from all others.

Trusting that you will excuse me for thus trepassing on your time,

I remain with high regard and
respectfull consideration
Very truly yours
R. Patterson.

PERSIFOR F. SMITH TO WILLIAM WALKER

Fort Leavenworth, Kansas
Territory, January 8' 1857.

General W. Walker
    President of Nicuaragua
        General

Nothing but an imperitive obligation of Justice induces me to address you with the view of aiding Major P. G. T. Beau-

109

regard in his design of establishing himself in the military
service of Nicaragua, under your authority. The loss to the
United States and especially to their army is irreparable when
he quits it—he does not leave his superior behind in any branch
of the Science of War, & if there were any hope that a position
in conformity with his merit could be attained here I should
feel myself bound as a citizen of the United States rather to
obstruct than aid his wish to join you. Major Beauregard is a
native of Louisiana, a graduate of the United States Military
Academy & now an officer of the U. S. Corps of Engineers.
He served through war with Mexico in the field & some of the
most important Engineering operations were committed to
him. He was in nearly all the action under Gen. Scott—in those
preceeding the Capture of the City & the occupation of it he
was attached to my Staff and I have a right to speak of him
from close personal observation. His merit is not confined to
excellence in his own specific Staff duties. He is equally distinguished as a gallant soldier, fearless, active & bold & would
gain laurels at the head even of an army.

He was wounded several times during the day before our
entry into the City but never intermitted his duties for a moment. In fact there is no position in the Army—including that
of Commander in Chief—which he is not qualified to fill and
I look upon the probability of his quitting our service as the
greatest loss that can happen to the Army.

There is no position that can be offered to him that
he is not better qualified to fulfil than any other officer I
know.

Excuse me then General if I present Major Beauregard to
you as an acquisition to your service such as cannot be surpassed
—and recommend him to your consideration with the most
perfect confidence of his possessing in an eminent degree

Appendix

every quality that goes to make the soldier & the gentleman.
With sincere good wishes & with the highest respect

Your obedient Servant
Persifor F. Smith.
Bt. Majr. Genl. U. S. A.

PERSIFOR F. SMITH TO BEAUREGARD

Fort Leavenworth Jany 8' 1857.

Dear Beauregard

We are almost entirely cut off from the rest of the country by the interruption of the mails— The river being closed with ice travellers are obliged to take the Stage & as they pay—the mails are thrown out to accomodate them— Yesterday brought up a wagon load of bags that had been left along the road & I hasten to send you the letter to Walker tho I fear it will reach you late as I can hear of no private opportunity of sending it to Jefferson City where the rail-road ends.

I assure you dear Beauregard that I think your quitting our service as the greatest calamity that can befall the army & the country. Let me assure you with sincerity that I know no officer left behind that can replace you if we get into an important war.

Let me beg of you too before you resign to visit Nicuaragua, see Walker and judge for yourself. I cannot for a moment entertain the idea of your serving under him— He is every way your inferior and indeed I do not think him equal to great emergencies.[2] He is personally courageous, but cold hearted & I think selfish, of contracted intellect so that he is deficient in resources in time of great need—he will consequently use no

[2] Smith's evaluation of Walker was an unusually shrewd piece of character analysis. It was also grimly prophetic. Beauregard was fortunate that he did not join Walker. Eventually the dictator's plans miscarried, and in 1860 he was shot by a firing squad in Honduras.

111

means but *"attack"* & when his strength is wasted for want of foresight—he then has no remedy but *"sauve qui peut."* & he will not hesitate to do all to secure his *own* safety regardless of his comrades— This is the judgment I formed of his character from my acquaintance with him in New Orleans—but especially afterwards in California— There I formed something like the same opinion of him from his principal adherents in Nicuaragua—they are all men far below mediocrity & some absolutely wanting in the characteristics of a gentleman.

For God's sake dear Beauregard do not resign until you have seen with your own eyes & tested by your own judgment.

I do not mean to accuse Walker of treachery or wanton deceit—but that his calibre is too small for the events he is called upon to control & he will be led by them into difficulties from which he will see no outlet but escape.

The persons in the U. S. who have embarked in this matter have, many of them done it as a speculation & they will not hesitate to deceive by false representations— Do not trust anything but what you see & learn yourself. Whatever you decide on—be assured of my heartiest & warmest good wishes & that you may count on me with perfect confidence under all circumstances.

Your warm friend & obedt Sert.

Persifor F. Smith

U. S. A.

Index

Abercrombie, John J., 36–37
Armistead, Lewis A., 82
Arnold, Lewis G., 30
Atalaya, 12, 13, 34, 38–39
Ayers, George W., 33
Ayotla, 14, 41, 44

Barnard, John G., 83
Beauregard, P. G. T., writes account of experiences in Mexican War, 3–5; grievances against General Scott, 4, 13–14, 21; at West Point, 6; decides to become a soldier, 6; in service in Louisiana, 6–7; admiration of Napoleon, 6, 19; joins American army in Mexico, 7; at Tampico, 7; at Vera Cruz, 11, 26–30; at battle of Cerro Gordo, 12–13, 33–39; reconnoiters around El Penon, 15; at the Pedregal, 15–16; at battle of Contreras, 16–17, 47–59; scouts approaches to Mexico City, 18, 60–67; at Piedad council, 19, 68–72; at battle of Chapultepec, 19–20, 75–83; in advance on Mexico City, 20–21; at Belen *garita*, 20, 84–96; military characteristics of, 21; opinion of Scott, 21, 104; at El Penon, 41–46; and capture of Mexico City, 97–104; decides to take service with William Walker, 106–112

Belen *garita*, 20, 84–96
Benjamin, Calvin, 90–91
Biddle, Charles, 82
Brooks, Horace, 27
Brooks, W. T. H., 33, 37, 54

Cadwalader, George, at battle of Contreras, 16, 49–52; at Piedad council, 69
Canby, E. R. S., 42–43, 54
Cape Anton Lizardo, 10, 25
Casey, Silas, 61
Cerro Gordo, battle of, 12–13, 33–39
Chapultepec, Mexican fortress, 18–19; battle of, 19–20, 75–83
Churubusco, battle of, 17
Claiborne, J. F. H., 4
Contreras, battle of, 16–17, 47–59
Coppée, Henry, 88, 95
Cuyler, John M., 53

Duncan, James, 15; at El Penon, 44–46
Drum, Simon H., 33; at Belen *garita*, 90–91

El Penon, 14–15, 41–46
Engineer Company, members of, 9; role in Mexican War, 9; at Vera Cruz, 10–11; Scott's opinion of, 78

113

Index

Index

Index